"Our world sees pain and suffering [as] circumstances. It is true that God d[oes not] suffering for us, but he does choose to work through them. Our God met Peter Mutabazi in the midst of his agony, and he will meet you in yours too. In fact, he will be with you—in plenty and in want—no matter what your situation. Read *Now I Am Known* and be encouraged."

Kyle Idleman, bestselling author of *Not a Fan* and *One at a Time*

"Filled with detail and imagery from his years growing up in Africa to his adulthood in America, Peter's astounding and unlikely true story proves that if you remain committed and give it your all, great things will happen. Even though our stories are different, I can relate to Peter as a parent and as someone who has had to put in the work. Reaching goals, pursuing happiness, and achieving a dream are not done without sacrifices, dedication, focus, and faith."

Sanya Richards-Ross, Olympic gold medalist, world champion athlete, and founder of MommiNation

"The pain of this tale runs deep, but its beauty and hope run even deeper. It is one of the most redemptive stories you'll ever read. Peter helps us feel the matchless ache of a child wounded by those who should have protected. Even more, he helps us to feel the matchless goodness present when a child grasps that they are valued and known through the tangible hospitality of a welcoming home."

Jedd Medefind, president of Christian Alliance for Orphans

"Peter's story takes us through pain and brutality, but it also shines with unexpected, life-changing hope. His touching journey will inspire and rekindle your own faith."

Raymond Arroyo, #1 *New York Times* bestselling author

"Peter Mutabazi's *Now I Am Known* is one of the most powerful books I've read in a long time. With heart and vulnerability, Mutabazi shares the seemingly insurmountable challenges of his childhood and how the power of connection with one person who believed in him offered him a chance to reimagine his story. *Now I Am Known* offers a vivid and true picture of the grace of God and will challenge most Christians' understanding of compassion, risk, and second chances."

Matthew Paul Turner, #1 *New York Times* bestselling author

"Filled with stories of heartache and tenacity, *Now I Am Known* calls each of us out of apathy and into action. Beware: Peter's words will grab you and beg you to risk it all by choosing bravery and love, even and especially when it costs you."

Manda Carpenter, foster parent and author of *Soul Care to Save Your Life*

"I will never forget hearing Peter's story for the first time around a dimly lit dinner table in a restaurant outside of Nairobi, Kenya. I was captivated, in awe, and inspired by the resilience of this man and the kindness of others who had so beautifully interceded on his behalf. And now, some years later, this same man has opened his heart, his home, and his entire life to do for other kids the very thing that so many people had done for him. I'm still captivated, in awe, and inspired. *Now I Am Known* will no doubt leave you feeling the same."

Jason Johnson, author of *ReFraming Foster Care*

"Peter is burdened for all children, and *Now I Am Known* tells the story behind his passion. As a fellow advocate for foster care and adoption, I can't say enough good things about the inspiration found in this book or the work Peter Mutabazi does every day. This book brought me to tears in the best kind of way."

Jen Lilley, actress and foster care and adoption services advocate

"Abuse can create monsters. It can also create compassionate individuals with a strong sense of right and wrong. I'm deeply inspired by Peter's kindness despite the intense abuse he and his mother and siblings suffered. This book is a must-read for anyone wondering whether they can actually make a real difference in this world."

Kelly Slater, American pro surfer and world champion

"Peter's story is such an amazing picture of the adopting heart of the Father and the way that he rescues us to be a part of the rescue mission. His story will break your heart and encourage you at the same time that God is active right now and making all things new. I pray this book will open the eyes of the church to the opportunity we have in our own communities to change lives eternally through foster care and adoption."

Joby Martin, pastor, The Church of Eleven22

"Peter's life is one of the most extraordinary examples of restoration and redemption coming out of dire beginnings. He has been the single most influential voice on my life to begin the fostering journey—and after these pages, you'll see why. *Now I Am Known* is a guttural, inspiring, honest, and no-fluff account of a heartbroken son growing into a powerful father. All because of choice and hope. A must-read for all those needing to find hope in their own chapters of life."

Carrie Lloyd, author of *The Noble Renaissance* and host of *The Carrie On* podcast

"*Now I Am Known* shares the I-don't-want-to-believe-it's-true story of an abused and abandoned kid without help or hope in the gutters of Africa who becomes a force of change and influence in the lives of hundreds of thousands of children. I know Peter personally and could not recommend his book more highly. You'll be inspired, encouraged, challenged, and changed."

Jason Shepperd, founder of the Church Project

"Peter's compelling life story is filled with many sorrows and heartaches, yet it is a reflection of God's amazing grace. Peter grew up in extreme poverty, and you can see God restoring his life in abundant ways and divinely orchestrating his plan to bring redemption to Peter's pain. After so many challenges in his young life, Peter easily could have chosen a path of bitterness and anger, but instead he decided to live out grace and forgiveness toward those who hurt him. Peter is a living example of God's great love, grace, and mercy to a broken world."

Greg Yancey, bivocational pastor, Mountain View Community Church, Fort Collins, Colorado

"Peter is a living legend. For anyone needing reasons to believe that their future is never limited by their past, *Now I Am Known* will be absolutely life changing! Peter's story is shocking and miraculous, which makes this book the most encouraging book you have ever read. Buy it. Read it. And give it to everyone you love!"

Ray Johnston, senior pastor, Bayside Church of Granite Bay, California

"Peter's story is a nightmare transformed into a dream come true. He is a true gift from God. His story is page turning, death defying, grace infused, and emotionally inspiring. This is truth stranger than fiction and a movie waiting to be made. But you will want to read his story first—it's that good. And he is as genuine in real life as he seems in the book. I count it an honor to be his friend. He is the real deal."

Ray Hardee, lead pastor and cultural architect,
The Pointe Church, North Carolina

"Peter is a classic example of God at work. Throughout Peter's life, he has had tribulations, but God was always present, showering him with hope. His book is a lesson on encouragement for all of us, and Peter articulates clearly that our circumstances do not define us. Instead, our faith in Jesus Christ is our salvation. Peter's compassion for those who are struggling and his willingness to bless them are striking. His incredible perseverance to become a father and break a generation of hardship and poverty is real and very touching."

Rodney A. McLauchlan, chairman of the board
at Legacy Trust Company

"Peter Mutabazi has endured it all. Name something terrible, crazy, and absolutely random, and this guy has probably lived through it. But he didn't let the pain of his circumstances end him. *Now I Am Known* is a story of hope that reminds us that whatever we might face today, it is not the end. Peter's is a modern-day Joseph story. We can begin over and over again—for ourselves, for our kids, and for our communities."

Nate Butler, songwriter, recording artist,
and music producer

"An amazing story of perseverance, servanthood, and the love of people. The world would be changed forever with this model of love, service, and discipleship in the Lord's name."

Lars Petersen Jr., founding elder, The Church of Eleven22

"I pray that Peter's story takes everyone who reads it to that breaking point where they experience the Holy Spirit changing their world."

Brad Veazey, MD, founder and CEO of Artis iQ

"In a world filled with an abundance of words and little movement toward action, Peter Mutabazi's story stands out. This is a man whose life has been so changed by God's love, he is compelled to put that love into action. In the twenty years that I've known Peter, he has been an encouraging friend, a wise mentor, and a man of integrity. And though I've heard Peter talk about his life many times over the years, in reading *Now I Am Known*, I am filled with renewed gratitude for his friendship and renewed wonder that someone who has had so much taken from him still has so much to give. This book is not only an inspiring story of perseverance through immense sorrow and pain but also a miraculous example of overwhelming hope and joy."

Derek Breuninger, carpenter, Kaiser Permanente

NOW I AM
known

How a Street Kid Turned Foster Dad Found

ACCEPTANCE and TRUE WORTH

PETER MUTABAZI

WITH MARK TABB

BakerBooks

a division of Baker Publishing Group

Grand Rapids, Michigan

Published by Baker Books
a division of Baker Publishing Group
PO Box 6287, Grand Rapids, MI 49516-6287
www.bakerbooks.com

Printed in the United States of America

Library of Congress Cataloging-in-Publication Data
Names: Mutabazi, Peter, author. | Tabb, Mark A., other.
Title: Now I am known : how a street kid turned foster dad found acceptance and true worth / Peter Mutabazi with Mark Tabb, Mark Tabb.
Description: Grand Rapids, MI : Baker Books, a division of Baker Publishing Group, [2022]
Identifiers: LCCN 2021061091 | ISBN 9781540901989 (paperback) | ISBN 9781540902238 (casebound) | ISBN 9781493437443 (ebook)
Subjects: LCSH: Fathers—Uganda. | Foster parents—Uganda. | Uganda—Social conditions.
Classification: LCC HQ756 .M8166 2022 | DDC 306.874/2096761—dc23/eng/20220216
LC record available at https://lccn.loc.gov/2021061091

The proprietor is represented by the literary agency of Bourland Strategic Advisors.

Baker Publishing Group publications use paper produced from sustainable forestry practices and post-consumer waste whenever possible.

23 24 25 26 27 28   7 6 5 4 3 2

To every vulnerable human being
who may not think there is hope,
you are seen, you are heard, you are loved.

Contents

one

My Power Within

The vine came down on me so fast I did not have time to duck. It ripped across my right arm and burned like fire. "You worthless piece of . . ." my father yelled as he swung the vine around like a bullwhip. I spun around to protect my face. "Don't you turn away from me." He grabbed my shoulder with his left hand, turned me around, and brought the vine down across my neck and chest. Out of the corner of my eye I saw my aunts, uncles, and cousins running out of their houses. They had come not to stop my father but to watch. Nyabikoni was a very small village. This passed for entertainment.

"What did I do?" I cried. I didn't expect an answer. My father never had to have a reason for beating me. Most days the sound of my breathing was enough to set him off.

"What did you do?! What did you do?! How dare you question me!" He hit me again and again and again until I fell to the ground.

"Stop, oh please stop."

"I'll stop when I'm ready to stop!"

I twisted and turned as the vine slashed across my skin. By now, all the shops on our street had emptied out. I saw my friends off to one side. No one looked surprised. In Uganda, a man can beat his wife and children and no one cares. It's a man's business, since it is his household. Besides, everyone in our village probably thought I deserved it.

Finally, my father's arms must have grown tired because he gave me one last blow, dropped the vine, and growled, "Get in the house!" I struggled to get up. My body was on fire. Huge red welts swelled up on my arms and legs. I recognized the vine lying on the ground. My father had beaten me with the Ugandan equivalent of poison ivy.

Once my dad turned around and stormed off to go drinking with his buddies at the local bar, my mother came over to help me up. "I'm so sorry, Peter," she whispered. "I'm so, so sorry."

"It's okay, Mom. It's not your fault." I did not blame my mother for not rushing to help me. My father beat her even more than he beat me. If she had tried to stop him, he would have turned on her. I knew that. My mother knew that.

"Come inside," she said. "I'll help you get cleaned up."

My mother knew the routine. My father beat me and my siblings at least four times a week. Everything we did threw him into a rage. One night he yelled at me to bring his socks, but then he took a swing at me for bringing them to him too slowly or too fast or for grabbing the wrong pair. He never had to have a reason for lashing out at us.

While the physical abuse happened every other day, the verbal abuse came every moment of every day. "You're garbage . . . I wish you'd never been born . . . I wish you were dead . . . A dog is worth more than you because at least a dog is good for something. You are absolutely good for nothing . . ." Every day of my life I heard some combination of these words, all of them punctuated with the f-word. By the time I was four, I saw myself through the eyes of my father. I believed I was useless. I believed I was garbage. I believed I had no reason for being alive. Many children dream about what they are going to be when they grow up, but not in my family. When I was ten years old, I'd given up on life.

I think my father was always angry because he never wanted this family. He and my mother came from different tribes that never intermarried. Somehow they still got together, and my mom became pregnant with me. That was never the plan for either of them. When my mother's family discovered she was going to have a baby, they drove her away. With no other place to go, she went to live with my father in his village near the Rwandan border. It was my father's responsibility to take in my mother because she was having his child. No one celebrated their "coming together," just like no one other than my mother celebrated my arrival a few months later. My father's family never accepted my mother or me or any of the children who came after me, and neither did my dad. He lived with my mother out of obligation, and they stayed together for the same reason. He took a job at a local medical clinic to support us, but he hated being tied down to this newly formed family. Most of all, I think he hated me because I reminded him of the life he never wanted and the life he would never have.

By the time my father returned home later that night, I was trying to sleep on the dirt floor of the bedroom of our two-room house. My brothers and sister and I did not have a bed of our own, but our parents did. The kids all squeezed together on the floor to try to stay warm, since we did not have a blanket or anything else to cover ourselves. I heard my mother open the front door, and my dad moved past her without saying a word. I closed my eyes and pretended to be asleep when he walked in. He ignored me and my siblings as he went straight to bed. Lying on the floor in the dark, I heard him recite the rosary before the room filled with his snoring.

We weren't so lucky the next night.

The Last Straw

The walls of our house were thin enough for me to hear my father walking outside. I listened closely to the sound of his steps to determine what kind of mood he was in. Tonight he stormed up the path to our house like a walking nuclear bomb. The moment he stepped inside he started yelling at my mother for not opening the door fast enough. Then I heard the pop of his open hand slapping her, then another and another and another. My mother cried, "The baby, the baby!" but the blows kept coming. "Stop, please stop," she pleaded. He ignored her just as he did every night when he beat my mother . . . or me. I lay on the dirt floor, angry at my father for abusing my pregnant mother and angry with myself because I could not do anything to help her.

I always wondered when my father was going to kill one of us. I knew he had it in him because I had witnessed it with my own eyes. Six months, maybe a year earlier, a man was caught stealing from one of our neighbors in the middle of the night. My father and a mob of men surrounded the thief and proceeded to kick and punch the man until he could not move. The man cried out for mercy, but the mob ignored him. Once the man stopped moving, my father helped tie him up and toss him in a back room of another neighbor's house. The next morning the thief's wife and her small children came looking for him. My father and the other men berated her, calling her the wife of a thief, although technically that was no longer true. By the time she showed up, she was already a widow. When the police arrived, they hauled off the body without asking anyone what had happened. Once they heard the man had been caught robbing a house, the police did not care how he died. This was how justice worked in our small village. The police were never there to protect. Villagers took matters into their own hands.

I cannot tell you how it feels to watch your own father join in with a mob to take a man's life. I do not think he and the other men intended to kill the thief. They were so enraged over what he had done that the group could not stop themselves. I knew it was only a question of when, not if, my father would be so enraged that he'd be unable to stop himself again.

"Peter!" my father yelled as he stopped beating my mother long enough to burst into the small room where I pretended to sleep. "Go get me some cigarettes." He then threw a little money at me as I scrambled to my feet, terrified.

"Yes, sir," I replied. I looked around the room to find my sweater.

"Now!" he screamed.

Thankfully, I quickly found my sweater and slipped it on over my T-shirt as I headed for the door. I hated going outside in the dark, especially this late at night. The sound of rain hitting our tin roof made my heart sink even deeper. Our village didn't have any streetlights. When the sun went down at 6:00, the only light came from the moon and stars above. Rain meant not even the moon was out—but the dogs and other animals were. The thought of running into a snarling dog made my knees shake, but facing an angry dog was better than what I knew awaited me when I returned home. Because of the rain, I had no way to keep my father's precious cigarettes dry on the half-mile walk back from the small store down the road. The beating my mother had just endured was nothing compared to what I knew my father would do to me when I walked back into our house with nothing but scraps of wet paper and tobacco.

Genesis of a Plan

The rain beat down on my head. The dirt road turned to mud. I reached down and felt the hem of my shorts. The little bulge was still there where I'd hidden my life savings. When you are poor, you have to be very resourceful to survive. Even though we did not have much, I discovered I could make money by selling handfuls of peanuts at a bus station a couple of miles from my house. As I walked down the dark, muddy road from my house toward the small shop that sold cigarettes, I started thinking about that bus station. I did not want to go back home. I could not endure the sound of my mother screaming for help and not being able to rescue her. I could not listen to my father berate me and tell me how worthless I was. And I could not take another beating. I hated my father so much that if we'd had a gun in our house, I would have used it on him. It was that or wait for him to kill me.

Even with all these thoughts running through my head, I still stopped at the house with the small store in the front and knocked. Although it was around three in the morning, a door still opened. The shopkeeper was used to people stopping by every hour of the day and night to buy moonshine. I walked in and bought a handful of cigarettes for my father. In a village like ours, you never bought anything by the pack. Instead, these shops sold nearly everything by the piece.

When I walked back out into the rain with the cigarettes, I looked back down the road toward my house. *If I am going to die*, I thought to myself, *I would rather die at the hand of a stranger in some far-off place than at the hand of my own father.* I turned and hurried the opposite way toward the bus station. My normal fear of walking alone in the dark grew exponentially, not because a dog might jump out at me but because every little sound might be my father coming after me, angry that I'd taken too long to get home with his cigarettes. I stopped walking and started running. I had to get far away fast. I did not realize it at the time, but this was my first step toward taking power over my own life. It would not be the last.

Escape

"Of all the buses, which one goes the farthest?" I asked a lady selling tea outside the bus station.

"That one," she said, pointing. I was relieved she didn't ask why such a small boy was out alone in the middle of the night. Maybe she'd given up on life as well. Hope was hard to come by in Uganda. When I was born, Idi Amin ruled the country through terror. Even though Tanzania drove Amin into exile in 1979, eight years under the "Butcher of Uganda" devastated our nation. Most everyone was poor. The economy was a wreck. At least half a million people died or simply disappeared while he was in power. Of course, I didn't understand any of this back then, but I did recognize the hopelessness that enveloped the world I knew.

"Thank you," I said before running over to the bus she'd pointed out. I didn't have to buy a ticket to get on board. Instead, bus drivers collected the bus fare after they'd driven far enough from the station that you had to pay up or be stranded in the middle of nowhere. Thankfully, I had enough money with me to reach the end of its line. I didn't know where the end might be, but I didn't care as long as it was a long way from Nyabikoni.

A handful of people were already seated when I climbed on the bus. I found a seat in the back and huddled down where no one could see me. Time slowed to a crawl. Every time I heard a man's voice I ducked out of sight just in case it might be my father looking for me. More people boarded the bus. Many carried bunches of bananas or bags of grain to sell somewhere far off. In Uganda, buses doubled as trucks for carrying goods from the rural areas to the cities. When I sold peanuts at the bus station, I even saw people carry goats and chickens onto buses. No one thought this was odd. It was simply life in my village.

I don't know how long it took for the bus driver to start the bus and get moving. Honestly, it might have been only thirty minutes, but for me, it felt like hours passed. Finally, the bus driver started the engine, and the bus moved out of the station. I peeked out the window, expecting to see my father, angry, looking to beat me for not coming back with his cigarettes. He had to wonder where I was . . . or did he? Did he even care I had not returned home? Did he hope the dogs had gotten me? He might look for me if he thought I was dead alongside the road. In Uganda, society judges you for how you take care of your dead. I wanted my father to be judged harshly. I wanted to rob him of the satisfaction of seeing my dead body and placing me in the ground. I'd rather be eaten by dogs.

The bus drove out onto the main road. *Finally*, I thought. We sped up but soon slowed to a crawl. I pushed with all my might on the back of the seat in front of me, thinking that I could somehow force the bus farther down the road, but no matter how hard I pushed, the bus didn't speed up. Suddenly, the entire bus swung wildly from side to side before speeding up. A few minutes later, the bus slowed back to a crawl. Once again, I pushed hard against the seat. *Why are we slowing down?* A car went by. I just knew my father had to be in that car. But the car kept going and the bus inched forward. Again, it swung so hard from side to side that I nearly hit my head against the window. Then we sped up again. Eventually, I realized the bus driver kept slowing down to avoid the huge potholes that pocketed the dirt road that doubled as a highway.

First Taste of Freedom

The sun had not yet come up when the bus pulled into another village. We stopped. I dropped down in my seat. I heard a man's voice. It had to be my father. Another man spoke. I also thought he had to be my father. But I never heard anyone yell my name. More people got on the bus. Most of the seats were now taken. A woman sat down next to me. She smiled at me, but I did not say a word. I could not take the chance that she might report me as a runaway. After a few minutes, the bus driver started the bus and we moved on down the road. At the next stop, a man took the last seat in our three-seat row. He sort of glanced at me, but I didn't make eye contact with him. *What if my father sent him to find me?* I pushed back in my seat where he couldn't get a good look at me. Finally, the bus started again. I let out a sigh of relief.

Half an hour later, the bus stopped again in the middle of nowhere. The bus driver got up and started walking toward me. "Who is going to Mbarara?" A few people spoke up. The bus driver went over to them and put out his hand. "Seven hundred shillings." They paid him. "Okay. Who's going to Kampala?" I raised my hand along with several people. "One thousand shillings," he said.

The bus driver went up and down the aisle collecting money. He came to me. The bus driver ignored me and spoke to the woman sitting next to me. "Two thousand shillings."

"What?" she said.

"Two thousand, for you and your child."

The woman looked at me. "He's not my child."

"I'm not her child," I said.

The bus driver gave me a suspicious look. "Okay. A thousand shillings each." He looked at me like he didn't believe I had that kind of money. I pulled several bills from the hem of my shorts and counted out one thousand shillings and placed it in his hand. "Hmm," he said, surprised. I smiled. It felt good to pay my own way.

Morning turned into day. My stomach started growling, which was normal for me. My mother had enough food to feed herself and my brothers and sister and me only every other day. My father never missed a meal, however. He always had money to buy food and alcohol for himself. He could have fed the rest of us every day. Withholding food was just another way he controlled our lives.

The bus pulled into another village. A wonderful smell came in the window that made my mouth water. I looked out and saw a man selling grilled chicken on a stick along with roasted corn on the cob. "Hey," I called out the window, "I'll take some."

The man walked over to my window. I pulled the rest of my money out of the hem of my shorts and hoped I had enough. Thankfully, I did. I handed the money down to him, and he gave me what turned out to be the best meal I'd ever had. And the best part was I didn't have to share it with my brothers and sister. Every bite belonged to me. This was probably the biggest meal I'd eaten in my entire life.

Unfortunately, I didn't realize what eating a large meal in a swaying bus along bumpy dirt roads with diesel exhaust streaming in the window would do to me until my stomach started gurgling. I tried to hold the food in, but the more the bus swayed, the sicker I felt until I stuck my head out the window and lost it. Yet not even throwing up could take away the satisfaction I felt over being able to buy a meal for myself. No one had the power to keep food away from me any longer. For the first time in my short life, I started to feel free.

The bus trip dragged on. The land became flat, which, for a boy growing up in the mountains, was something I'd never seen. Short grass and acacia trees stretched out forever in every direction. All at once a woman a couple of rows in front of me yelled, "Oh my! Look at that!" Everyone in the bus stood up and stared out the window. *What are they looking at?* I wondered. I stuck my head up. A giraffe stood right next to the bus. I gasped. In school, we sang songs about giraffes and read about them in books, but now one was so close I felt like I could reach out and touch it. *Am I dreaming?*

"Over there!" a man yelled. I whipped my head around, but I could not see a thing. Other people began oohing and aahing. *What do they see?* More people jumped up and pointed out the window. "Can you believe that?" someone said.

"What?" I said.

"I hope they don't charge the bus," a kid said.

"Nah, they're too far away," a man replied.

What is it? I wondered. I kept looking around until finally I looked out farther from the bus and I saw it, a bull elephant. My eyes grew wide. Even though it was nearly a mile from the bus, it was still huge. Then the elephant began moving, and I saw a herd of maybe seven or ten or twelve elephants moving along behind it. I was too excited to count the exact number.

I stared off into the distance, wondering what else I might see. Gazelles pranced along like they were moving from one acacia tree to another. I caught a glimpse of a zebra. Right then I did not care about my father or my village or where I was going. All I wanted to do was stay here and take in these incredible sights I never knew existed in the real world. For the first time, I was glad the bus had to crawl along the pothole-covered road. "What is this place?" I asked the woman next to me.

"The national park," she replied.

"Wow. I wish we could stay here."

The woman laughed. "I'm sure you do."

Eventually, the animals disappeared as the bus kept moving closer to the next village. The sun started back down in the sky. My father had to be home from work by now. He always came home before heading to the bar. Once the sky grew black, I knew he'd probably left the house to go out drinking. One time I happened to see my father in his favorite bar with his friends. I did not recognize this man. He had a huge smile on his face, and he was actually laughing. I didn't know he could be anything but angry. But the sight of him happy and enjoying himself made me hate him more.

Staring out into the night from the bus window, I also thought about my mother. My heart broke. My mother loved me so much, and she had to be very worried about me. I hated putting her through more pain when she already lived with so much. Most days I helped her around the house. By the age of seven, I could run the household like an adult. My happiest times came when I got to work in the garden with her. While digging sweet potatoes or picking beans and peas, she told me stories of her village and her life before she met my father. I wished I could have known her then, back when she was filled with happiness and optimism about her life. But she did not have that option any longer. In small villages of Uganda in those days, women were less than second-class citizens. My siblings and I belonged to our father, and he could do whatever he wanted to us. And to her. When my father erupted in anger toward me, my mother could not stop him. However, many times she put herself between him and me, taking my beating for me. I longed for the day when I would be big enough to protect her from him, but I doubted I would survive long enough. Enduring a beating myself was bad enough, but watching him abuse the one person I loved the most in this world was more than I could take.

Kampala

The scenery outside the bus changed again. Lit-up shops and houses lined both sides of the road. The bus slowed down again, but instead of crawling over potholes, we crept along with the traffic that surrounded us. In Nyabikoni, a car or two might come through our town in a day. Here, cars filled the streets, pushing their way through crowds of people who spilled off the sidewalks into the road. Horns honked, people yelled, chaos ruled. I had attended elementary school for only three years, and even then I rarely went every day or even every week, but I had enough schooling to know that Kampala was the capital of Uganda and our largest city. This had to be it. Where else on earth could there be a city this large?

The bus turned down one road, then another. I looked out the window and saw kids racing after us, yelling, waving their hands. *Why are they out so late? It has to be close to midnight.* The bus pulled into a crowded station. We stopped. The kids who had been chasing the bus jumped up and down outside, calling to people through the windows. I had no idea what they were saying. Every once in a while I heard a few words of English that I recognized from school.

Everyone on the bus got up and gathered their possessions. No one stayed seated, no one but me. People began to exit. As they did, kids rushed on and helped carry the bags of grain and bunches of bananas. I stayed stuck in my seat, wide-eyed. I noticed one kid helping a man with a bunch of bananas pull one off the bunch and toss it back on the seat without the man noticing. When the kid saw me staring at him, he gave me a quick nod like he knew exactly what he was doing.

The last passenger left the bus. The bus driver came back to me. "This is it, kid. Time to get off."

"To where?" For the past fourteen hours, I'd thought about nothing but getting as far away as I could from my father. Not once did I think about where I was going, only where I had been.

"I don't know, but it can't be here," he said.

I hesitated.

"Now, kid."

I got up and slowly started walking to the door of the bus. This was the end of the line. I had no idea what to do or where to go, but I knew one thing: having nowhere to go was better than going back to my father. I took one last look back at my seat and stepped out into the chaos of the bus station. As I did, I felt something I had never felt before. It would be decades before I could identify that feeling—a sense of freedom and power. I had survived a nightmare. I no longer had to sleep with one eye open or one ear open. I somehow had mustered up the courage to forge my own path, less fearful of whatever lay ahead for me than what I had left behind.

Catching that bus to Kampala was my ticket to hope, and it was the beginning of learning to see myself differently. I no longer see myself as useless, worthless, or a burden; although, I do require the occasional reminder. Many of us do. We have traumas or heartaches that have stunted our emotional development and capacity to heal. We carry the injustice throughout our lives, never achieving our full potential. We settle for surviving. I wanted more for myself, just as I want more for my children and foster children and for everyone reading my story. Sometimes that first step is seeking freedom in the midst of fear. For me, it meant leaving that toxic environment in order to get a view of what a true and hope-filled future could look like. Before you can be known by others, you have to leave places, patterns, and ideas that lie about and devalue who you are. My hope is that you will find the power within yourself to take that first, brave step.

two

Survival Mode

The bus terminal emptied as the crowds wandered off into the night. I kept an eye on the group of boys who had helped people carry their belongings off the bus. Now that the bus was empty, they went back over to it and started talking to the bus driver. A couple of the guys looked my way, and we made eye contact. One motioned to me to join them, like they actually belonged in this place. Something about them made me think I could trust them, at least a little.

One of the boys said something, but I had no idea what. I think he may have been speaking Swahili, which is one of the most common languages in Uganda, or maybe it was Luganda, the tribal language of Kampala. I did not yet know how to distinguish between the two. I mainly spoke Runkiga, the tribal language of my village, and Kiga, which was my mother's tribal language, and Kinyarwanda, which is the official language of Rwanda and regions on its borders like my home village. I also knew a little English from school, but not enough to carry on a conversation.

While I was trying to figure out what the boy had just said, some of the boys spread out around the bus and began wiping it down with rags. "Do you want to help us?" the boy asked in a dialect that was close enough to Kinyarwanda for me to understand.

I nodded. Everyone understands a nod. He motioned for me to follow him back onto my bus. My new friend pointed at the food wrappers under the seats and gave me a look that said, "You know what to do." I nodded and got down on the floor and gathered up all the trash I could reach. I rose with my arms full. I looked at my friend. His arms were full with the plantains and beans other boys had left behind when they had carried the passengers' things off the bus. The boy motioned toward the bus door. Outside I noticed a trash pile growing on the far side away from the buses. I followed another kid and dumped my trash on the pile. I later learned the bus companies have no one to clean the buses between trips. Street kids do it in exchange for the bus drivers overlooking the fact that most of the helpers also help themselves to a little of the passengers' cargo.

After we cleaned the bus, the other kids brought whatever food they'd gathered over to the trash pile. Someone had already started a fire, over which they roasted the plantains they had taken from the bus. I stuck close to the boy I sort of understood. He walked over to the fire and took a couple of roasted plantains. I started to follow but stopped myself. I was hungry, but I did not know if I was allowed to eat or whom to ask. No one seemed to be in charge, yet everyone but me knew what was going on. I sat back, trying to figure out how to get some food when my friend came back over to me. "For you," he said and handed me a plantain.

"Thank you," I said.

He smiled and nodded as if to say, "No problem."

I had no idea how hungry I was until I took that first bite of the plantain. How long had it been since I'd eaten the chicken and corn? It didn't matter since I'd thrown it all up on the bus. Another boy who looked to be a couple of years older than me came over. He said something, but I didn't know what. The boy who gave me the plantain answered. The other boy nodded and looked at me. He said something else. My friend turned to me and said, "What's your name?"

I hesitated. Telling them my name was Peter didn't feel right. My parents gave me that name, but nothing good had ever come of it. I was in a new place. A new name seemed appropriate. My mother, not my father, gave me the last name Habyarimana,[1] which means "a gift given to me by God." With my father's approval, she gave me my name when I turned two, because in Uganda you waited to give a child their full name until you were sure they were going to survive. I didn't care much about what the name meant, but since my mother gave the name to me, I thought I should keep it. Habyarimana is way too long for anyone to remember, so I said, "Call me Habi."[2]

"Habi," the boy I could not understand repeated with a nod and a thumbs-up. For the next four years, no one ever called me anything but Habi.

Once we finished eating, I wondered where we might sleep. The answer was: we didn't. Not that night or really any night during my years of living around the bus station. To survive on the streets, your antenna has to be on high alert 24/7. The same defensive nature I had formed with keeping an eye out for my father, I now put to good use on the streets. Something as simple as a man walking toward you could turn into this same man kicking you in the head just for the fun of it. I'd rather not sleep. I went as many as five days without sleeping at all. When I hit a wall and could not keep my eyes open any longer, I slept half an hour or forty-five minutes at the most and usually in the middle of the day. Since we stayed near the garbage piles, the flies made it difficult to rest. The moment I drifted off, they attacked, crawling up my nose, into my ears, and around my eyes. Flies were worse during the day, but that was the safest time to rest. When everyone else was busy, they paid little attention to a kid lying on his back covered with flies in a small piece of shade.

I had not yet learned those lessons the first night. My body felt very, very tired, since I had gone nearly two days without sleep. But then the sun started coming up, and people spilled back into the bus station. Only then did I see that this was far more than a bus station. Small shops popped up, and they sold everything. Some shops sold fruits and vegetables, while others sold staples like flour, rice, and sugar. There were spice shops and candy shops and shops that sold baby clothes and others that sold women's and men's clothes. You could find shops filled with radios and other electronics. You could even find a shop with parts for your car. Basically, all the small shops turned the area around the bus station into a giant, open-air market, and once customers showed up, it was a thousand times crazier than any market you will find in the Western world. It was like living at a flea market and a state fair all at once. I forgot about being tired.

The boys spread out through the bus station and marketplace. A well-dressed white man came along carrying a suitcase. One of our boys went up to him, said a few words, then grabbed his suitcase and followed along beside him toward one of the buses. The man got on the bus, and the boy came back carrying a small bag of nuts. Another boy hung close to one of the produce stands. A woman with a small child paid for some plantains and tomatoes. Before she handed over her money to the shopkeeper, the boy asked her something. I then watched as he carried her bags to a car. She handed him a couple of plantains before driving off. The boy who shared his plantains with me approached a man buying some clothes at one of the shops. When the boy asked a question, the shopkeeper chased him off. My friend came over to me and said something like, "We will get him later."

After watching my group, I walked into the crowd and started working. Most everyone coming to the bus station area knew what I wanted when I approached them without me having to say a word. If I had to say anything, I knew enough English to say, "Help you?" and "Food" while raising my hand to my mouth. It didn't take long to figure out who to approach and who to leave alone. Women with small children gave the most food. Priests in clerical collars and nuns always gave something. White people did too. Seeing white people was a new experience for me. Not many made it to Nyabikoni. My friend told me later that any white person who came down to this marketplace was probably a missionary.

Not everyone was so generous. Some of the people I approached cursed and yelled at me like I was a stray dog. I guess that's what I and all the other street kids were, strays.

At least we were strays together. I'd been in Kampala for less than a day, but I'd found a place where I fit in with a group of boys who helped one another survive. I guess you could say I'd found a sort of family, one I was eager to join because I was so desperate not to be alone. Within four weeks, I picked up enough Luganda to communicate with my new family. Once we could communicate, I learned this family was very different.

Detached

I would not have survived my first few weeks on the street if not for the street kids who let me join their group. They taught me how to get food, where to go and where not to go, how to hide from the police, and which people to approach for help and which to avoid completely. But their help came with a price. Begging for food never brought in enough to feed everyone, even though we all shared equally. And that's where I came in. My new family needed me to steal what we couldn't get by begging.

Before arriving in Kampala at the age of ten, I'd never stolen anything. Back home, everyone struggled to get by. Taking something from one of our neighbors was unthinkable. Even worse, if I got caught, shame would fall on my family. But I no longer lived in my home village. The only thing left to fear was getting caught, but since I was young and small and new on the streets, the stakes weren't as high for me. If caught, I might be yelled at or beaten, but the shop owners had harsher penalties for the teenage boys. I once saw an angry group of shop owners stuff a grown-up thief into a car tire. They then doused the man and the tire with gasoline and set him on fire. No one stepped up to stop them, and the police never showed up because they usually avoided the bus terminals. The shop owners didn't need the police, not when they had tires and gasoline to hand out justice. Setting a man on fire sent a message to everyone else: if you are going to steal, you might not survive to see another day. But when you are hungry enough, it's a risk worth taking.

I thought my heart was going to beat out of my chest the first time I moved close to one of the produce stands to help myself to a banana. A crowd of people huddled around the stand. A small woman asked how much the tomatoes were while an older man haggled with the shop owner over the price of melons. I moved over to the side of the woman, reached up, and pulled a banana off a pile. Before anyone could see what I was up to, another boy walked past and I slipped the banana into his hand. He then passed it to another boy who passed it to another like a moving shell game until the banana had passed through so many hands that no one outside our group had any idea where it might be.

My second time stealing came a little easier. I carried an older man's bags of produce to his car. The moment he turned his back to open his trunk, I helped myself to a piece of fruit out of one of his bags. By the time the man turned back around, the fruit had already disappeared into thin air. The man had no idea I had taken anything. He reached into his bag and gave me some food for helping him. I walked away feeling quite proud of myself for pulling off a double dip. We all ate a little better that night because of me.

After a while, helping myself to whatever someone else might own did not even feel wrong. We had nothing. The shops, shoppers, and travelers had something. Either they could share with me or I'd take what I wanted or both. My friends and I needed food, and we did whatever we had to do to survive.

Survival meant everything because I lived in a world where death was a normal part of life. Even back in my home village, people got sick and died so often that it did not seem strange when death came. They died from disease. They died from AIDS. They died from accidents. I lost grandparents. I lost many aunts and uncles and cousins. I even lost my brother who was maybe a year younger than me when I was only nine. I was the one who found his body. It was his day to fetch water, but when he didn't return for a long time, my mother sent me to check on him. That's when I found him, facedown in a small pool of water, dead. He had epilepsy. My father never took him to the doctor for medicine that might have helped him. Instead, when my brother went into a seizure, we tried to make him comfortable until it stopped. On this day, my brother had a seizure and no one was around to catch him before he fell into the water. By the time I found him, it was too late. I rushed back home and got my mom. We carried my brother's body back to our house, where my family washed him and prepared his body to be buried while men from our village built a coffin behind our house to give him an honorable burial. In our village, the way we cared for our dead said everything about our family and our reputation in the community. The next day friends and family came to mourn him. The same men who built the coffin dug his grave. On the day of the funeral, I was distraught. My mother was too. To my surprise, I actually saw my father shed a tear over my brother. I had never seen him cry before, and I've never seen him cry since.

On the streets, death was even more common. Some days a boy in our group would lie down and never wake up. Others just disappeared. When we did not see them for a couple of days, we assumed they were dead. One of my friends died when a man threw acid on him. Others died after eating something they thought was food that turned out to be poison. Drunks sometimes came through and beat up a street kid so badly that he died. On hot days, we sometimes crawled under buses to get out of the sun. If a boy fell asleep, or if he wasn't paying attention when the bus started to move, the bus rolled right over him. When a person didn't die immediately, the rest of us had no way to help them. No doctor ever came to the bus station, and no ambulances ever rushed in for a disposable street kid. Instead, we sat and watched our friend die, all the while knowing that we could be next. After a friend died, the rest of us still had to go out to scrounge and steal and do whatever we had to do to survive. We could not wait around for the authorities to haul away the body. In Uganda, someone's family was supposed to take care of their body after they died, but that didn't apply to street kids. No one mourned when one of us died. To others, our lives didn't matter. And to the many people rushing past, we weren't even human, which only reinforced everything my father had ever said to me. However, now I could walk away or retaliate without caring about what might come next.

After losing a couple of boys I had grown close to, I learned I had to become calloused and detach myself completely from everyone and everything if I was going to survive. That's probably why in four years on the streets of Kampala none of the other street kids ever asked me about my home village or my family, and I never asked anyone about theirs. We told stories and we joked around when we could, but all of us made sure we never got to know anyone too deeply. The odds were good that one day I'd have to watch a friend die or he'd have to watch me. I did my best not to think too much about that.

We may have stayed detached from one another, but in our own strange way, we were still a family. If we didn't look out for each other, no one else would, and there was a lot to look out for. If someone hurt one of our family members, we made sure we paid them back. I was a boy, and I was small for my age. Most of the kids on the street were. We couldn't threaten people to their faces. Instead, we found passive yet effective ways to retaliate against those who crossed us. If we spent a lot of time carrying produce for a farmer and helped him set up his shop but he stiffed us, we made sure no one bought anything he had to sell. Defecating in the middle of his tomatoes had a way of keeping people away. In the same way, if a farmer was extra nice and paid us well for our help, we protected him and made sure no one stole from him. That let people know not to mess with our group. We also watched those who came to the marketplace by car. If someone was mean to us or did something to hurt one of our guys, that person soon found one of his tires slashed or missing altogether when he went to drive home. Again, that was our way of letting everyone know that we may have been only a bunch of kids, but we had the power to protect ourselves. I never felt bad about retaliation. I had to have a hard heart to make it.

Losing Faith in Humanity and Myself

In my years on the street, I quickly learned not to trust anyone but one of my guys. I wish I had a stronger way to say
this. I lost more than the ability to trust. I lost faith in humanity. No one ever did anything without wanting something
in return. We had nothing to give but ourselves, and people
knew it. They took advantage of our desperation. I learned
this lesson as I got older. There were women who had their
own shops in the marketplace. One started treating me well.
She even gave me food. She made me think, *Maybe I was
wrong about people after all. Maybe there are some who
are genuinely kind.* Those thoughts didn't last. A day or two
later, this same woman demanded sexual favors from me
of a kind I never imagined having to give. But I was hungry
and she offered me food, so I did what she asked and tried
not to think too much about it later. At least I had food for
that day. I wish I could say this was an isolated event, but it
wasn't, nor was I the only street kid who had to prostitute
themselves for food. We didn't talk about it. We just did
what we had to do.

A lot of kids also used drugs to cope with life on the street.
Marijuana was popular, but I never touched it. I didn't neces-
sarily have a moral objection to it. I didn't touch it because
my dad smoked, and I refused to do anything remotely close
to what my dad did. A few times someone in our group
scrounged up alcohol, but I avoided that as well. My dad
drank every night, which was reason enough for me not to
drink either. I did, however, join in with sniffing diesel. I'd
stuff part of my shirt into a truck gas tank, pull it out, and
hold it under my nose and breathe in. Some kids did this

to get high, but I had another reason. To keep people from bothering us, we street kids lived near a garbage heap next to a drainage ditch. Since the bus station and marketplace did not have public toilets, most people relieved themselves in the drainage ditch. Dead animals also had a way of ending up there. Uganda sits on the equator, which means it is hot and humid twelve months a year. Put all that together and you end up with a stench I cannot put into words. Diesel fumes smelled a lot better than the combination of decaying garbage, urine, human feces, and rotting animals.

While I longed to get away from that smell, I had nowhere else to go. Eventually, I felt like this was where I belonged. When you live around garbage and you smell like garbage and people treat you like garbage, it's hard not to think of yourself that way. I had no dreams for the future. None of us did. None of us ever thought beyond the present day. We could not afford to consider the future, let alone dream about it. The moment you started thinking too far ahead, acid could come flying at you or a bus could come barreling your way.

That's what it means to live in survival mode. You live in the moment. You trust no one but yourself. You do whatever you have to do to see another day. It isn't living. It's hardly surviving. You lose any sense of being human. You have no empathy, no compassion, no faith, no kindness. It's hard to give what you never receive.

Thankfully, my story did not end there. Thanks to the unexpected kindness of strangers, which you will soon read about, I survived those experiences and came out on the other side. I now have extreme empathy for anyone who's experiencing tough times and may not feel like their life matters. I understand what it means to steel your emotions while at the same time trying to survive. Life can be gritty and complex. Our life journeys are far from being direct lines to happiness. Sometimes it's all we can do to take each hour, each day as it comes, and that's okay. It's been a long time since I lived in survival mode, but I have carried some of its lessons with me for a lifetime. Having faith, taking it easy on myself, and being okay with not passing judgment on my situation or others have freed me from trying to earn love and prove my value by living perfectly. Because of that, I reach deep to extend empathy and to encourage others as often as I can. We must choose to see others as people doing their best rather than judge them at their worst. Life is hard. We all need to give ourselves, and those around us, a little grace.

three

Seeking Happiness

After I had been in Kampala just over three years, I approached a man in the marketplace and asked if I could help him carry his packages in exchange for food. I do not remember if he said yes or no because the moment he replied to me, I forgot all about food. "Wait," I said, "you speak Runkiga?" I had heard maybe two or three people speak my native language since I had run away from home.

The man was as surprised as I was. "Yes," he said.

"So do I," I said. The man was a stranger, but finding someone who spoke the same language as I did pulled me out of the stench of the bus station for a moment. He asked where I was from. I told him Nyabikoni.

"Nyabikoni? That is where I am from," he said.

"You're kidding." It had been a long time since I'd run into anyone from my village. Every once in a while someone came through the bus station. That's how I was able to let my mother know I was alive not long after I arrived in Kampala. I didn't want her worrying about me.

"I live here now," the man said, "but that's also where I am from." He studied my face. "You look like someone I know."

"Who?" I asked.

He told me my father's name.

Hearing that name made me want to cut off the conversation right then, but before I could walk away, he said, "You have a close relative here in the city. Perhaps I can arrange for you to see her." "Close" is a subjective term on the continent of Africa. Here in America, most people I know consider a close relative to be an aunt or uncle or first cousin. In Uganda, "close" may be ten relatives removed. The distance does not matter; family is family.

Even then, I was skeptical about meeting anyone related to my father. Now that I was free from him, the last thing I wanted was to get myself entangled with anyone connected to him. "Yeah, I don't know," I said.

The man did not press me. He did, however, give me some food, which I appreciated. Before he left, he said, "I know where you work. If you ever want to see your auntie, let me know."

To Be Known

I saw this man in the marketplace a few times over the next couple of months. He usually told me that the offer still stood to meet my relative if I changed my mind. I thanked him and told me I'd think about it. I kept hustling food, stealing what I needed, sleeping from time to time, watching friends disappear and die, wondering when my time might come. In other words, business as usual. Then one day the man came and found me. "I talked to your relative," he said, "and she really wants to meet you."

Maybe the streets were getting to me, or maybe it was hearing that someone actually wanted to meet me that changed my mind. Either way, I told him I wanted to meet this long-lost relative. We arranged a time, and he showed up to take me to her house. I did not know what to expect of her home. My parents' house in my village was very small with a dirt floor and a tin roof. While I had not ventured too far away from the bus station in my years around Kampala and I certainly had not been in anyone's house, I had seen many beautiful homes on the drive into the city years earlier. I wondered if perhaps my relative lived in a place like that.

She did not.

Today, the section of Kampala where my relative lived has been transformed into gated communities filled with beautiful multimillion-dollar homes. Not then. To me, the neighborhood looked like someone had tried to cram as many tin-roofed shacks with mud walls as possible into the smallest space imaginable. I followed the man down a narrow road crowded with drunks and prostitutes and their customers. Music spilled out of more bars than I could count. The man and I moved quickly, diligently watching everyone around us. We turned one corner in time to see a brawl break out. "You have to be careful around here," the man said. By the time we found my relative's house, I wished I had not agreed to see her.

The moment my relative laid eyes on me, she threw her arms around me. After nearly suffocating me in her hug, she pulled back and looked at me like I was a long-lost son.

"Peter," she said, which was the first time anyone had called me by my given name in a very long time, "Oh, Peter, it is so good to finally meet you. I am your aunt Maria."[1] Technically, Maria wasn't my aunt, since she was not the sister of either my mother or my father. However, in Africa, "aunt" refers to any older relative connected to you by tribe. Since Maria was in her late forties or maybe her early fifties, she qualified.

I told her I was glad to meet her as well, but my mind stayed on high alert. In spite of her warm welcome, I had no idea if I could trust this person. I noticed a man sitting in a corner. "This is my boyfriend," Aunt Maria said. "He stays here sometimes." *Great*, I thought, *one more person to watch out for.*

We had a small meal, after which Aunt Maria said, "Peter, the streets are no place for a boy like you. I want you to come live with me."

I should have jumped at this opportunity, but instead I asked, "Can I think about it first?" My aunt did not want to take no for an answer. She told me she could not bear the thought of me living out on the streets another night. I started to give in, but I was not sure I could live with someone related to my father. I also did not want to start staying with her that night. If I did, my guys back on the streets might think the man I had left with had done something to me. The next time he showed up at the bus station, he'd be in big trouble. I did not want that to happen.

When I went back to the bus station, I could not stop thinking about my aunt's offer. She may not have lived in the best part of town, but at least she lived in a house. Even a house in the worst part of town beat sleeping next to a garbage heap. My aunt also did not have much, but one meal a day, or even one meal every other day, was better than stealing bits of food here and there.

But the biggest factor that made moving in with my aunt Maria attractive had nothing to do with food or shelter. She knew my family. She knew my background. She wanted to know me. With her, I was more than a nuisance of a street kid whom nobody would miss if I did not wake up one day. I was Peter Habyarimana. I had a name, and that made me feel a little more human when I was around her. Something inside me craved to be known more than anything in this world. The next time I saw the man who took me to her house I told him I was ready to leave the streets and have a home again.

No Place like Home

Aunt Maria welcomed me like the child she never had. She fussed over me and cooked for me and brought me treats from roadside food stands. Although her entire house was maybe ten feet by twelve feet, I had my own space to sleep with a roof over my head. I did not have to worry about someone attacking me while I slept. Given the circumstances in which my aunt lived, I was as safe and comfortable as I possibly could be. I actually began to believe that perhaps life did not have to be day after day of pure survival. My aunt was so kind and so loving that I felt a glimmer of hope for humanity. All my life I had seen the worst in people, but now I actually saw some good. *Maybe I can find happiness here*, I thought.

My aunt had never raised a child before. At times she was a little overprotective. Anytime I left the house she peppered me with questions: "Where are you going? Who are you going to be with? How long will you be gone?" After living for years with no rules and no authority over me, I didn't like having to answer to someone. However, once I got to know her schedule, I had no trouble slipping around her rules. Most days I stayed at her house and did nothing, but sometimes I snuck out and went back to hang out with my friends on the streets. The bus station did not seem far. Looking back, it could have been ten miles away, but for a street kid who was used to walking everywhere, ten miles was nothing.

I really wanted to be happy in Aunt Maria's house. I told myself that living with her was the best place for me. However, no matter how hard I tried to convince myself, the trauma that drove me to run away from home three years earlier came back to overwhelm me. My aunt was not the problem. She genuinely loved me and wanted the best for me. Unfortunately, she had lived and worked so long in this part of the city filled with drugs and prostitution, drinking and violence that it felt normal to her. She even played a part in it all. My aunt Maria sold moonshine at all hours of the day or night out of her house. Most of the drunks knocking on her door reeked of cigarette smoke. The sound of their voices as they demanded something to drink took me right back to my father coming in drunk after a night of drinking with his friends. It took me right back to that state of high alert in a home where all I wanted was to feel safe.

I might have been able to suffer through the drunks at the door, but that was not the worst of it. In many ways, the slum was worse than what I saw living on the streets. No one here cared about anyone but themselves. Outside of my aunt, I never witnessed one act of compassion, not one instance of someone coming to the aid of another human being. Whenever the day came that I would become a victim, no one would care about me either. I was no longer a street kid, but my life held no value in the eyes of the people in the shacks next door or down the street. The neighborhood lived by the law of the jungle. Kill or be killed. Take or be taken. Eventually, my turn would come.

Nights were the worst. All the houses in this part of town were pressed together with thin, common walls of mud between them. The tin roof overhead did not have any sort of insulation to keep out sound. Instead, all the noise from the entire neighborhood sounded like it was in the same room with me. Every night I heard the drunks fighting in the streets. I heard the prostitutes and their clients doing business. But the worst were the cries of prostitutes as their clients beat them. Every cry of every woman rekindled the trauma of listening to my mother being beaten by my father. I heard the men yelling in anger or laughing in sick delight as the women cried for mercy, and I thought, *So this is what all men are really like?* Before I had a slim hope that maybe my father was the exception, but now I knew he was not.

One night in particular threw me over the edge. As I lay on my bed, trying to sleep, an argument started. The voices were so loud that the people had to be right next door. A man demanded services, but the woman asked for her money to be paid first. The man refused. When she asked for the money again, I heard a loud slap. She screamed. She told him to get out. Another slap. He started to curse, calling the woman every name in the book. With every curse came another slap, then a punch, then a kick. The woman cried out in the night for help. No one came. No one ever came to help the prostitutes when they were in trouble. The more she cried, the angrier the man grew and the more severe the beating became.

I lay on my bed, paralyzed. I went right back to the night I ran away from home. Just like that night, part of me wanted to jump up, find the man, and beat him as severely as he was beating this poor woman, but I knew there was nothing I could do. I was too small, too powerless. Perhaps if I had my friends with me, together we could do something, but I didn't. By the time I got them, it would be too late. I thought about running outside and yelling for help, but everyone in the neighborhood could hear what was happening, just like they heard the same sort of abuse every night, and no one ever did anything. In Uganda at that time, no one thought anything of a man abusing a woman, especially a prostitute. I refused to accept this as okay behavior, but I was afraid that if I lived in this world long enough, I'd become completely numb to the suffering of others. After all, what made me think I was any better than anyone else?

Finally, the woman stopped crying. The man yelled something at her before storming out her door. I listened closely for the woman's voice, hoping to hear some signs of life coming from her house, but I never did. The next morning my worst fears were confirmed. I walked outside and watched as someone carried a woman's body away from a nearby house. Men passed by. I looked deep into their faces. I wondered if one of these was the man who had killed her, but there was no way to tell for sure. They all had the same expression on their faces, the same one I saw on my father so many times, an expression that told the world that he was in control and no one better cross him.

Right then and there I decided that no matter how many meals my aunt Maria prepared for me, no matter how much she cared for me, I could not stay. I waited a day or two before telling her that I was leaving. I thought she might not let me go if I told her I was going to go back to the streets, so I thanked her for all she had done for me over the two months I had lived with her, which I sincerely meant, and told her that I was going to go home to my mother and father. She cried when I said I was leaving, but she assured me that she was very happy I was going home. "This city is no place for a boy like you," she said. She gave me money for the bus fare back home and walked me to the bus station. I did not have the heart to tell her the truth. Instead, I hugged her goodbye, then climbed onto a bus and waited until she left. Then I jumped off and went right back to the life I had lived before. Life on the streets had not changed, but I decided I'd rather take my chances there, where my fate was in my own hands, rather than live in a place where behavior like my dad's was the norm. I could not live with the thought that someday I might be like him.

Try. Fail. Try.

Even though I ended up leaving my aunt's house, I have no regrets over my decision to move in with her. She was the first person other than my mother to show me kindness and love. I wish I could have stayed with her. I wish being in her neighborhood had not thrown me back into the trauma I had endured from my father. But I knew I had to leave, and yet, Aunt Maria's love for me gave me my first glimpse of hope that perhaps I could find a better life, that perhaps all people were not the same. I had given up on life and given up on the human race. Aunt Maria lived in a place where she easily could have done the same. She was surrounded by violence and hostility and the worst of humanity. Yet, from the moment she met me, she loved me. Perhaps there were others out there like her. I hoped that was true.

Once my life turned around and I was in school, on my way to a better life, I went back to see her. I don't remember if I ever admitted the truth about what happened after I left. The subject may never have come up because she was so happy to see what I was doing with my life.

Several years later, while I was a university student, I was able to pay back her kindness when she passed away. As I wrote earlier, in Uganda, the way you honor those who have passed says a lot about your own character. When word came to me that my aunt had died, I gladly accepted those responsibilities. I paid all her funeral expenses and even escorted her body back to my home village for burial. This was not my first trip back there, but it was the first time I was able to show my family, and especially my father, that I was a man of honor, that I cared about people and treated them the way I wanted them to treat me. I knew if the roles had been reversed, Aunt Maria would have done the same for me.

I also learned a valuable life lesson through the experience of my two months with my aunt. When I went to live with her, I thought I had found my escape. I thought I had found a safe place, but sadly, I had not. Living there brought me back to the trauma I had experienced from my father. I had lived through a lot more trauma on the streets, but suffering abuse at the hands of a stranger does not compare to suffering abuse from one who is supposed to love you. I found that

I could more easily compartmentalize abuse from strangers. I had deep pain over the fact that the one who should have been my protector had no interest in my emotional or physical well-being.

From these days, I learned that finding goodness and happiness takes a lot of attempts. Try. Fail. Try again and again and again for as long as it takes. We cannot give up on the first or even second attempt at happiness. If we keep fighting, we will journey to a better place. Even the process of trying and saying, "I will" guides us to recognizing strength and goodness. I have seen adults give up when fighting their own demons or trying to break the chain of addiction. It is important that we all rally around one another, cheering each other on to better days and fulfilled dreams.

four

Surprised by Kindness

They say never to judge a book by its cover, but to survive on the streets you have to. If a man or woman came into the marketplace wearing worn-out shoes, that told me they walked everywhere and could not afford a taxi. I learned not to ask someone like that for food because they probably did not have enough for themselves. But if someone drove to the marketplace in a car, that meant they had money. The nicer the car, the more money they had. A beat-up car with a driver in old clothes told me they might give me some food but not to count on it. Someone driving a nice car in nice clothes might not "give" me anything, but I knew they had enough that I could help myself to a little of whatever they had.

One day not long after I returned to living on the streets, I spotted a man walking through the market wearing a nice shirt, eyeglasses, and khaki pants. Someone dressed like this did not walk to the marketplace. He had to have a car. However, what he was wearing did not stand out as much to me as his height. The man was shorter than most adult men, probably a couple of inches or more under five feet tall. A short man meant he had short arms, and short arms meant he needed help carrying whatever he bought in the market. Since he was well-dressed, this was a guy who was going to give me all I needed whether he realized it or not.

I followed the man, keeping my distance and planning my approach. The man moved through the marketplace like he was in an American supermarket. Not once did he check over his shoulder or put his hand on his wallet to make sure it was there. *This guy doesn't have a clue*, I laughed to myself. Easy marks like this guy didn't come along very often. I followed him to a produce stand. The man picked up a bunch of plantains. I crept closer. Timing was everything. I had to be quick and aggressive without appearing too aggressive if I was going to obtain food for myself and my friends.

I made my move when he laid the plantains down to pay for them and took out his wallet. I don't think he even knew I was close by when I stepped over and picked up his items to carry them back to his car. To my surprise, before I could get any words out, he looked at me, smiled, and said, "Okay, let's go." *Perfect*, I thought.

"All right," I said. We reached his car, and it was a nice one, a Land Cruiser or something like that. I thought to myself, *Okay, this is someone who will not miss whatever I take*.

But before I could steal anything, or even ask for a handout, the man peeled off a couple of the plantains and handed them to me. He looked at me and smiled. "What's your name?"

In all my years of living on the streets, no one had ever asked me my name. I was okay with that. Anonymity helped me forget myself and remain calloused, detached. Hiding my actual identity helped me dissociate. I lived behind the illusion that Habi controlled my body while Peter kept himself at a safe distance.

On the other hand, something about the way this short man asked my name stirred up an unfamiliar hope inside me. He asked like he cared about more than my name. It was as if he cared about me. His question made me feel like I had been lost in the wilderness for years, alone, when I happened upon another human being for the first time and heard them say hello. The man asking my name made me feel like he did not see me as a nuisance or a beggar or a piece of garbage thrown out into the street. He saw me as a fellow human being.

"Peter," I said before I could stop myself.

"Thanks for the help, Peter. I appreciate it," he said as he climbed into his car.

I walked away feeling vulnerable, like I had opened a door that I should have kept locked. I steeled myself against worrying or thinking too much about it. *So he knows my name. What can he do with that? He gave me food. That's all that matters.*

A week later, I saw the same Land Cruiser in the parking area. I looked around and spotted the man at one of the farmers' shops. "Hey, James,[1] how are you today?" the farmer said when the man walked up to him.

James, okay, that's good to know, I thought. Since he knew my name, it only seemed right that I should know his. *Maybe I can get another free meal out of him.* However, before I could get close enough to grab his stuff, another street kid stepped in to help him. I went to his Land Cruiser, thinking he might give me a little food if he recognized me. When I got closer to the car, I heard two kids laughing and talking inside it. I peeked in an open window on one side of the car. "Hi," a boy said. The other, a girl, smiled and said, "What's your name?"

"Peter," I replied.

James walked up. Instead of asking what I was doing talking to his children, he said, "Hey, Peter, do you like nuts?"

I nodded, a little bit in shock. I cannot tell you how unusual it was for someone to be kind to me more than once. In my experience, no one ever did anything kind without demanding something in return. I was not sure how to receive his kindness. Part of me felt as if a breath of fresh air had just broken through the stench of the bus station, like I could actually breathe again. However, deep down, I also stayed suspicious. *Watch out, it's coming,* my mind told me. *The abuse will follow; it's just a matter of time.*

James gave me a couple handfuls of nuts before getting in his car and driving away. As the car pulled away, his kids in the back seat smiled and waved. The sight of two children being happy in the presence of their father was also new to me. There had to be something different about this guy.

Another week passed. I saw the same Land Cruiser pull into the parking lot. This time a woman got out. I assumed she had to be James's wife. I was disappointed that James wasn't there to give me food. I followed the woman and hurried to help her while she paid for her things. At the car, she turned and gave me a couple of bananas.

The fourth week came. James returned to the marketplace right on schedule. Once again, I helped him and he gave me food without me having to ask. More than that, he started a conversation with me like two normal people meeting at the market. After that, whenever James came back to the market, my friends called out to me, "Hey, Habi. Your buddy is here." Because many of us street kids shared our food with one another, if one of us built a bond with someone, the rest of us backed off and did not try to get in on the action. The stronger the bond, the more generous the person became and the more food all of us enjoyed. None of us ever considered anyone outside our group a friend. James was a nice guy, but that did not mean I trusted him. He was simply a routine food supply who didn't demand anything from me . . . yet.

To the Moon

Months went by, maybe a year or more. (Since every day felt exactly like every other day, it was hard to keep track of time. Sundays stood out only because the marketplace did not open and very few people came to the bus station.) James, his wife, and their family came to the marketplace like clockwork every other week and sometimes once a week. Every time he came he spoke to me and gave me food. I thought this was a pretty good deal. When you live in survival mode, finding a consistent food source lets you know you can make it through another twenty-four hours.

One day James showed up just like he did every week. I walked with him through the marketplace and carried his stuff for him just like I did every week. On our way back to the car, he turned to me and asked a question no one had ever asked before. "Peter, you are a smart kid. If you had the opportunity to go to school, would you go?"

I smiled, but not because I wanted to go to school. I smiled to try to keep from bursting out laughing because this had to be a joke. I had no shoes. I had nowhere to sleep. My clothes were practically rags. *School? Would I want to go to school? Oh, sure. Why not ask me if I want to go to the moon? Of course I want to go to the moon. Sign me up. When do we leave?* A street kid going to school was just as likely as one of us being recruited by NASA.

I held in my laugh long enough to say, "School? Sure, I'd love to go to school." I hoped my answer put an end to this conversation. I didn't have time to deal with this kind of over-the-top idea because I had a much darker reality to navigate every day.

"Okay. I'll see what I can do."

"Thank you," I said. *I can't wait to go. Ha!*

After that conversation, every time I saw James, I asked, "Hey, you mentioned school. When do I go?"—but not because I wanted to go. I did it simply to tell him what he wanted to hear. People who live in trauma do this all the time. We do or say what people want in the hope that they might give us what we need. My strategy worked with James—for months! I brought up school, and he gave me food. I was so happy with my strategy. I kept working this guy like I had never worked anyone else. I felt brilliant.

One day when we got to the car with James's market purchases, I asked again, "So when do I get to go to school?" I had to suppress a smile over how gullible he was at playing my game.

But on this day the game turned. "Today," James said, "if you are ready."

Whoa! I wasn't ready for that answer.

"I brought you clothes for school," James continued. "I'll wait while you go take a shower and change, then we'll head straight to the school."

I stopped in my tracks. *Shower. Did he really tell me to go take a shower?* When Marie Antoinette heard that the masses of French people did not have bread, legend tells us she responded, "Let them eat cake." The French people appreciated her comment about as much as I appreciated being told to go take a shower. All I could think was, *Where exactly do you expect me to find a shower? I sleep next to a garbage heap and a drainage ditch. Perhaps I can move the dead animals out of the way and bathe there. Is that what you have in mind? Or maybe you can do a rain dance and I'll strip right here and shower in the rain. Go take a shower?* This guy couldn't be this clueless. Maybe this was his plan all along, to turn me into a big joke he could laugh about with his family and friends.

James had to notice the look on my face. Before he could ask what was wrong, I just shook my head and walked away. I wanted to disappear as quickly as I could.

The next week one of my friends called out, "Hey, Habi. Your friend is back." I went over to James's car, but only because my guys depended on this food source. I hardly said a word to him, and I definitely did not bring up school. He did. "The offer still stands, Peter. Just let me know when you are ready." I grunted, put his groceries in his car, took some food, and got away from him. We did the same dance for a few months. I needed his food, but that did not mean I had to stick around and let him mock me.

Finally, after knowing James for nearly eighteen months, when I was about fifteen years old, he changed his tone.

"Peter," he said, "I am serious about taking you to school. It's a boarding school. They will give you a place to sleep and three meals every day starting today if you want to go. I have arranged everything. All I need you to do is clean up and change into some new clothes, and we can go there."

Three meals a day! To me, that sounded better than going to heaven and walking the streets of gold. In survival mode, nothing meant more than food. When I begged, I never asked for money, only food. When I stole, I stole only food, and maybe some clothes when I needed them to stay warm. But I could live without clothes. I could not live without food. I'd go anywhere if they promised to feed me.

Also, it may sound like I was being too sensitive, but when James said "clean up" instead of "shower," I knew he was not mocking me. Anyone can clean up. I could find some water to splash over my face and head and be ready to go. I wondered why he had not said this in the first place.

Still, I was a little suspicious of what James might really be after. In my experience, everyone looked out only for themselves. He had always treated me well, but that could change in an instant. The whole idea of him taking me some place where I'd get to eat all the food I wanted sounded too good to be true. There had to be a catch. Why would this stranger promise me heaven on earth? Part of me wondered if there really was a school.

"Okay," I said, still suspicious. He had been kind. He had fed me all this time. I could go with him to this supposed school and see what he really had in mind. I grabbed the clothes he brought and went to clean up. A couple of my friends came over and asked what was going on. I told them about the school, but I also added, "Look, I'm leaving with this guy. If you don't see me in twenty-four hours, burn this guy to death. Do to him what you will know he did to me."

"You know we will," one of them replied.

I changed into the new clothes, then went to find James. "Ready?" he asked.

"Yeah," I said. I followed him to his car and climbed in the back seat. I had known James for a year and a half and I was willing to give him twenty-four hours, but I planned to take notice of every street, turn, and landmark—anything I needed in order to get back to my street life.

At the same time, climbing into the back seat of his car was like stepping into a dream. It was calm. It was peaceful. I was comfortable. I had never ridden in a car before. I noticed, however, that as soon as James started the car, he rolled down every window. Perhaps I had not cleaned up quite as well as I thought I had.

"I have something else for you," James said and handed me a box.

I carefully lifted the lid to find a pair of blue and white Converse All Star sneakers. "Thanks," I said, unsure what else to say.

"Go ahead, try them on."

"Yeah . . . uh, right," I said. The shoes were beautiful. I can still picture them today. Sky-blue shoes with laces the whitest white I had ever seen. A round white patch with the distinctive blue star in the middle and the words "Converse All Star" popping out in red. I had no idea what "All Star" meant, but I didn't care. These shoes were like a work of art. If you had to have shoes, these looked like the coolest shoes in the world. But the thing was I had never worn shoes before. Kids in my village didn't wear shoes. Up until that moment, I had never felt the need to put on a pair.

"The school requires you to wear shoes. I thought you might like to start off with a new pair. Do you like them?" James said.

"Yes. Of course," I replied. I pulled the shoes out of the box and crammed my feet into them.

"Do they fit?" James asked.

"Yes. I think so."

"It may take a little time to get used to them," James said.

You can say that again, I thought. I kept them on to make James happy, but I planned to kick them off the first chance I got. To this day, I hate wearing shoes. I much prefer going barefoot. If I have to wear something, I choose to wear sandals.

Why Me?

The car ride seemed to take forever. We wound through the streets of Kampala, then followed a road outside the city. I watched everything and drew a map in my mind as we drove. No matter where we ended up, I knew I could get back to the bus station when I needed to.

However, one question burned in my mind throughout the entire two-hour drive. Finally, I had to ask, "Why me? Why did you go through all this trouble to put me in school?" I thought maybe James felt sorry for me and wanted me to have food and shelter. But if that were the case, what about the twenty or twenty-five other street kids I hung out with? Out of all these guys, why did he choose me?

"Because I can see that you have potential, Peter. You're a smart kid. I think you will do well in school," he replied.

Potential? Me? He had to be joking. *Potential? How?* All my life I had been told I was useless. Through my years of living on the streets, with few exceptions, nearly every adult I had ever encountered treated me like garbage. I did not matter. I did not have purpose. I did not have a life, just an existence. I certainly did not have a future. I did not believe I could do anything that might make tomorrow better than today.

But James saw in me something I was incapable of seeing in myself. That, more than taking me to school or any of the other wonderful things he did for me in the coming years, was the greatest gift he gave me. He looked beyond my filthy clothes, beyond my stench that I could no longer smell, beyond my dirty mouth and my anger and my constant attempts to sabotage his kindness because of my refusal to trust anyone. Rather than judge me for what he saw, he chose to believe that there was something in me that could be nurtured into a better life.

When James saw the good in me, I wasn't very good at doing that myself. Not just with myself but with everyone. I expected the worst in people, and I usually managed to find it. Even today, I must intentionally choose to look beyond behaviors and external circumstances and see the humanity within. As a father of four children ranging in age from five to seventeen, children who lived through extreme trauma before I became their father, I have to make this choice every day. When one of them explodes in anger over something as simple as being told it's time for bed, I have to look beyond the behavior and understand the root cause of the outburst. James did that with me. How can I not do that for my own children?

All of us can give this same gift to others, especially those who need it most. When life beats people down for too long, they lose hope. They cannot see a way out of their circumstances. They cannot see their own value. When others cannot see their own potential, we need to step in and see it for them. I know. My life was never the same after my first car ride.

We finally arrived at the school in time for lunch. When they gave me a tray in the dining hall, I had trouble believing all the food was just for me. In my entire life, I'd had exactly one meal that I did not have to share: the roasted chicken on a stick and corn on the cob I had bought on the bus ride from my village to Kampala five years earlier. After lunch, a couple of staff gave me a tour of the school and explained what life was going to be like for me there. As with the food, I had trouble believing they meant what they said, but I played along. This was all too good to be true.

Later, they told me it was time for dinner. I could still taste lunch, and it was time to eat again! Two meals in one day? I really had died and gone to heaven.

five

Is This Real?

When James first asked me about going to school, I thought he should have asked if I wanted to go to the moon, that's how ridiculous his question seemed to me. I had no idea how right I was. The moon could not have been any more different than Katweha Primary and Secondary School was to the only world I had ever known. Everything I saw, every smell, every building I entered, and every person I met sent my head spinning. Nothing felt familiar. *Am I even on the same planet?* I wondered. *This cannot be real. Places like this and people like this do not exist.* I felt like an alien stepping foot on a hostile planet. My brain screamed that I should get away from there as fast as I could, but these aliens gave me food. As much as I wanted. Three times a day. How could I leave that?

A Different World

When I first climbed out of James's Land Cruiser at Katweha, my nose didn't know what to make of the scents of flowers and cut grass and a fresh breeze blowing across the tree-covered hills surrounding the school grounds. Where was the diesel exhaust cloud? Did people not go to the bathroom around here because I couldn't smell urine and feces? I took another breath, trying to find the stench of rotting garbage and decaying animal carcasses. I had lived in filth so long that fresh air was a brand-new sensation, something I had not experienced since I had run away from home.

My eyes also went into shock. *Where is the trash?* I wondered. *Where are the plastic bags and crushed plastic bottles and food wrappers and rags encrusted with mud?* Everywhere I had been since I was ten years old, litter covered the ground, not just at the bus station but all over Kampala. Because it was a major city in a developing nation torn apart by war, no one thought anything of it. When I first moved to the United States, grocery store clerks asked if I wanted paper or plastic. Walk down any street in Kampala and the answer was both and lots of it. Paper and plastic and every other kind of debris were an everyday part of the landscape. But not at Katweha School. I did not see even as much as a gum wrapper lying on the ground. My brain was reeling. *How is this possible?* Instead of trash I saw green, lots and lots of green. From the neatly cut grass surrounding paved walkways between stucco buildings with red tile roofs to the bushes next to the buildings and the shade trees and palm trees that sprung up everywhere, I almost had trouble processing what I was seeing. After living in a monochrome world of gray at the bus terminal, seeing actual living plants felt very odd.

Then I toured the different buildings on campus. Every building had a purpose. The classroom buildings were very long. Rooms lined both sides of a central hallway with windows looking out on the school grounds. All of the primary classes were together, with the secondary in another building and the advanced in another still. Since Uganda uses the British system, the grades did not line up exactly with the American system, but at least there was a system. In all my years, I had never lived in any system other than "do what you have to do to survive no matter what it takes."

When I entered the boys' dorm, I had no idea what to expect. Back at the bus terminal, you slept wherever people might leave you alone. If the dorm had been like that, the whole place would have been one giant room with blankets tossed around every which way. Instead, the headmaster led me to a cubicle-type area with a door. Inside I found two sets of bunk beds along with four closets. "This is your room, Peter," he told me. "That bed," he said, pointing to one of the upper bunks, "is yours, and this closet over here is where you can keep your clothes and schoolbooks and the rest of your things." Both sets of beds looked alike, as did the other partitioned areas in the dorm. How was I supposed to remember which space was mine? And how could I possibly sleep up on top of a bed like that? What was going to keep me from falling out? I'd slept on dirt floors and under buses but never up off the ground. And certainly not as high as a bunk bed. I wasn't sure I'd be able to sleep between sheets on a springy mattress high above the floor. And I had lived without sleep for most of the past four years. "Lights are out from ten at night until six the next morning," the headmaster explained.

"Why?" I asked.

He smiled. "For sleeping, of course."

Eight hours of sleep in one day? That was a month's worth for me. How could I lie still for an entire night? After I slept, what was I supposed to do with the other seven and a half hours of darkness?

My first few nights I ended up with a full eight hours of darkness to fill. I tried lying on the bed, but I hated it. Every night of my life I'd slept on the ground. After tossing around trying to get comfortable on a mushy mattress for half the night, I climbed down and found a spot on the floor. But I still couldn't sleep. Not only were the lights out for eight hours, but they also kept the door closed. I felt like I was suffocating. I lay there, struggling to breathe, one thought racing through my head: *I have to get out of here!* I ran through a few scenarios of what I could do, but soon the lights came on and thirty minutes later I followed the rest of the boys to the dining hall for breakfast. Then came lunch. And dinner. If being locked in a dark room with three other boys for eight hours every night was the price I had to pay to eat three times a day, so be it.

Aliens

Eight hours for sleep was only one of many, many rules. They had rules for everything, from what we wore to where we could go to how we interacted with teachers. I had never understood rules. I grew up with a very strict father who tried to control every part of my life, but his "rules" were very inconsistent. My siblings and I simply had to do everything he said exactly the way he said it, but no matter what we did, we always ended up getting punished. Go fetch water. I fetched water. He beat me when I came home because I hadn't been quick enough or I spilled too much as I hurried back. No matter what I did, I could not please him. Dad made new rules for me every day, but to me, they were nothing but excuses for getting angry and beating one of us.

On the streets, we lived by one rule: survive. If I stole from a produce stand but no one caught me, good for me. When the rainy season came and I needed a jacket, I helped myself to one out of someone's bag. If they caught me, shame on me. But if they didn't, I had a way to stay warm in the rain and not get sick. I did what I had to do to stay alive, and I never asked permission from anyone to do anything.

But I no longer lived in that world. This new world at Katweha had lots of rules, and the other students not only followed them but also, as I learned on the first night, tried to make me follow them. As soon as the lights went out, I jumped up and headed for the door. One of the boys in my quad sat up. "What are you doing? No one is allowed out of our room after ten," he said.

"Says who? I have business I need to take care of," I said. I had to get back to my friends and tell them that James really had taken me to a school. If I didn't get word back to them right away, the next time they saw James he might not make it home alive.

"But the rule says . . ."

"The rule only means something if I get caught, and I won't get caught," I said and headed out the door. Honestly, I did not know what the big deal was. I got back early the next morning before anyone even knew I had left. The next night the same kid reminded me of the ten o'clock rule. I did not have anywhere I needed to go, but I almost left just to show him what I thought of his rules.

But there was no escaping the rules. Perhaps a thousand kids lived at Katweha School, and all of us had to wear the same neat, clean uniform. The boys all wore white shirts and khaki pants. The girls wore blue dresses with a belt around their waists. I had no idea how to tell anyone apart. Every boy looked like every other boy, and every girl looked like every other girl. *This is bad*, I thought. In the world from which I came, distinguishing one person from another was the difference between life and death. How else could you tell those who might give you food from those who might throw acid in your face?

The way the kids all moved about also came as a shock to my system. All my life I had lived in chaos, but in this school, kids walked down the hall in order. I looked into a classroom. I could hardly believe my eyes. Twenty-five or thirty kids all sat still, looking forward, listening quietly to the teacher as she taught. The kids talked, but only when the teacher asked a question.

Even when I attended the public school in Nyabikoni, pandemonium ruled. Teachers taught in English, but none of us understood English well enough to catch everything they said. Looking back, I wonder how much English those teachers knew. None were anywhere close to fluent. Yet they still taught in English, reading it off the pages of the books while a self-assigned student who understood that part of the lesson rattled off translations to those around them and each of us asked questions in our native tongue only to be translated into English to the teacher. It was noisy and crazy, but it was also the norm in my hometown school, where my parents paid a nominal fee—about $10—for me to attend three months of classes.

Katweha School was a boarding school and much more expensive, which made me think every child was wealthy. I later learned they were not rich or well-off. Most kids had parents who sacrificed to keep them in this school, which put pressure on the students to do well and make the most of their precious opportunity. Watching kids following all the rules as they sat still and listened, not speaking until asked, I thought they had to be some sort of mutants. They couldn't possibly be real human beings. Eventually, I caught on. After a few months, I slowly realized that Katweha established all the rules to protect the students. Once I understood the reason for each of their rules, I found it easier to go along like everyone else—at least most of the time.

What's the Catch?

The strangest characteristic of the kids, and especially the adults, was their kindness. The nicer everyone was, the more suspicious I grew. In my experience, no one ever did anything out of the goodness of their heart, because I had seen very little goodness in anyone's heart. I cannot tell you how many times while living on the streets an adult handed me a box of food with a big smile on their face like they were doing me the greatest favor in the world. I was so excited to receive food. "Thank you, thank you," I said . . . until I opened the box only to find rocks or rotten food with maggots. The moment I opened the box, the "kind" adult nearly fell over laughing at my reaction. I tried to keep from getting fooled. Instead of accepting any box, I watched to make sure the person offering it actually ate from it first. These "generous" adults weren't any better. Sure, they handed me the box of food, but all that was left were chicken bones or crumbs. Again, they'd laugh, like fooling starving children was the height of comedy.

The first time I ate in Katweha's dining hall I wondered what was wrong with the beans and peas and potatoes and plantains they served. Surely they would not give me something edible for free. But this food wasn't just edible. I felt like I had stepped into a five-star restaurant! On my way out, I asked the person in charge, "When is the next meal?"

"We serve dinner at six," she replied.

I had never paid attention to a clock. "How long is that?" I asked.

"When the sun goes down," she said with a smile.

When I went back to the dining hall at six, I expected to see a big "closed" sign. To my great surprise, I walked in and they gave me another plate filled with more beans and peas along with some sweet potatoes and a roasted plantain. On my way out, I asked the person in charge, "When is the next meal?"

"Breakfast is at six-thirty, or a short while after the sun comes up," she said with the same smile. I showed up the next morning still suspicious. I was given porridge and African cornbread. On the way out, I asked the same question and received the same gentle answer. I had the same conversation with this woman after every meal every day for weeks.

After a few weeks of receiving three meals each day, I finally decided this was not a joke. However, I still didn't let my guard down. There had to be a catch, and one Sunday I thought I'd figured it out. Katweha School was connected to a church. To stay at the school, I had to go to church. That was not a big deal to me because church held no meaning for me. My father claimed to be a staunch Roman Catholic, but he never let that get in the way of how he treated my mother or my siblings and me. My extended family was more of the same. I watched an auntie pray and repent, even weep before God on Sunday, only to see her go into a stranger's house for sex on Monday. I guess once she "got clean" with God she could then go out, mess up for six days, and return to church the next Sunday to repent again. I didn't see much point to that.

I attended the church connected to Katweha just as I was told. I sat through the service and went to Sunday school without complaining. I had done a lot worse in order to receive a free meal. Everything was cool until one of the adults told me I had to go play with the other children. *So that's it*, I thought, *here's the catch. You have decided to punish me.*

I nodded my head, noting that they wanted me to play with the others. Then I walked over to a corner of the churchyard and sat down, hoping to be left alone. My plan worked, but only temporarily. The longer I stayed at the school and the more times I went to church, the more I heard an adult tell me to go play with the other kids. Finally, one of the student counselors changed the command into a question. "Why aren't you playing, Peter?" she asked.

"Why don't you go ahead and beat me now?" I replied.

She gave me a very puzzled look. "Why would you say that?" she said.

I thought her response was just one more way to torment me. To me, the answer was obvious. Every time I had ever tried to act like a child and have fun, I had ended up being punished. My father had no patience for children playing. He yelled at us for making noise when we tried to goof around;

he shouted at us to do something useful for the family. There was always work to be done, like fetching water, going to the store for his cigarettes, helping my mother in the garden, or taking care of my brothers and sister. Once I arrived in Kampala, merely surviving meant there was no time to play. The idea of playing felt ridiculous to me.

All of that ran through my mind every time an adult at church told me to play with the other kids. Playtime equaled punishment. I did not confess this to any of the adults or this caring counselor. Instead, I just looked at her, waiting for the beating to begin.

She crouched down and looked me in the eye. "Peter, no one is going to beat you. You have potential. It is my job to help you see that. You have an amazing opportunity, and that is why you are here."

Potential? This was the second time an adult mentioned this word and linked it to my name. I did not know how they saw potential in me, but hearing it made me feel good inside. Maybe they were right. Maybe I did have potential, but for what? And then there was this word *opportunity.* I knew the definition, but I had no idea what she meant. The school was nothing more than an opportunity to eat every day and to live in a safe place away from city streets.

Still Surviving

Looking back, I honestly do not know why the school let me stay, especially after I got in a fight my second day. I had grabbed an extra potato during dinner and snuck it back to the dorm. Even though the woman in the cafeteria told me I would eat again at 6:30 the next morning, I didn't count on it. On the streets, when food is available, you take it instead of waiting for a meal that may never come. I did not know bringing food back to the dorm was against the rules, nor did I care. Food always came before rules. Always.

I dropped the potato on my bunk and headed to the bathroom. The same boy who warned me not to leave after lights out saw my potato lying on my bed while I was gone. In fear that we might all get punished for my action, he snatched it up and hid it before a dorm captain saw. However, he neglected to tell me what he had done.

I came out of the bathroom and went straight to my bed. "Who took it?" I said to the entire room. One kid pointed at the culprit. I walked to the guilty party and punched him right in the face without asking any questions. He tried to fight back, but he was no match for someone who had learned to fight on the streets. The rest of the boys jumped in and pulled us apart. Everyone looked at me wide-eyed like, *Whoa, who is this new kid?* And that's what I wanted them to think. I didn't fight over a potato because I was angry. I beat this kid up to let him—and everyone else—know not to mess with me or my stuff.

A day or two later, a kid caught me rummaging through his locker looking for a pencil. I needed one. I knew he had one, so I took it. When he walked up to me, he asked, "What are you doing?"

I didn't answer. Instead, I turned around and punched him in the face. I kept the pencil.

A few days later, I started a fight that almost ended in a fatal disaster. A student named Andrew crossed me, and I reacted like the streets had taught me. I went from zero to one hundred—straight into fight mode. I grabbed Andrew by the shirt and ran him across the room and threw him out the window. We were on the second floor, but I didn't care. I had a message to send, and the window was the quickest way to make him fear me. I might have killed Andrew if his shorts hadn't caught on the window frame and stopped him from falling out head first. A couple of guys pulled him out of the window while the rest of the boys jumped between us to stop the fight. Believe it or not, Andrew eventually became my best friend. Maybe that was his way of keeping me from throwing him out another window. Even though I liked Andrew, he could not treat me however he wanted. I did not fight out of anger. I fought out of self-preservation.

All the other boys should have hated me, and the school should have kicked me out, but they didn't. They tolerated my acclimation to the new environment, and eventually I figured out that if I stopped fighting and attended class, the school would continue feeding me and let me stay. My first several weeks I didn't even have to go *into* the classroom. I stood outside the window and listened to the lessons. The teachers let me observe and keep my distance. I do not know why, but they did. I had no idea why they did anything for me, but I wouldn't be here today if they hadn't taken me in gently and with consistency. The greatest gift the school administration, staff, and other students gave me was the gift of patience. They did not expect me to come off the city streets and suddenly act like everyone else. They let me be me and move at my own pace.

One of the greatest myths I run into today is that if we change someone's circumstances, we will automatically change their life. The idea is easy to believe—if you don't come from a hard place. The truth is trauma's impact lasts much longer than the trauma itself. It shapes you and impacts how you see and interact with the world. Simply removing someone from their source of trauma does not heal the mind, soul, or spirit. In spite of what some believe, love alone does not conquer all. Love must be dispensed with patience and kindness over long periods of time, and even then, we may never completely heal from trauma's effects.

If not for the grace I received from James and the faculty, staff, and students of Katweha, I shudder to think where my life may have ended up. I am fairly certain I would not be alive today. I would have been just one more faceless, nameless, dead street kid no one missed and no one remembered after he was gone. Instead, I received a future and a hope—the full extent of which I would not understand for years to come.

Grace is hard to give, especially when we think a person has already been given everything they need to succeed. That was me when I arrived at Katweha. I had a place to live, clothes to wear, and food to eat. More than that, I had a tremendous opportunity to receive an education and improve my status. But I couldn't see it. It's not that I chose not to see it. My mind simply could not comprehend what lay in front of me. If the school had thrown me out for fighting, most people would have looked at the lost opportunity as my fault—I threw it away—just like we castigate college athletes who come out of hard places but then get into trouble on campus and lose their scholarships. "They had the opportunity of a lifetime and they threw it away," people say in disgust.

When we look at people through that lens, we miss what's really going on and the deeper pain and sorrow underneath. Life beats up people. When that abuse comes early on, the impact lasts a lifetime. I see this in every foster child who enters my home. They do not know how to receive kindness and lash out instead. They may finally have landed in a safe place, but they still live in survival mode—self-preservation, hungry, untrusting. Like I did, when a foster child moves from an abusive situation to a peaceful household, they feel like they've landed on an alien planet. When you find yourself in that place, all you want to do is go back to a familiar place—"home"—even if home is hell. Hurting people do not deserve judgment. They need understanding. They need patience. They need love. They need grace.

six

First Flicker of Hope

One afternoon while I was watching kids play in the commons between our dormitories, a boy called to me, "Hey, Peter. We need one more guy for a football[1] game. What do you say?"

Almost as a reflex, I called back, "No, I don't think so."

"Oh, come on," he called back. "We need another guy or the teams won't be even."

"Sorry," I said.

"Have you ever played before? It will be fun. We'll show you," he said.

Had I ever played before? Of course I had. Every kid on the continent of Africa and in most of the world plays soccer, even if just on the playground. In my home village, we made soccer balls out of grass, banana fibers, trash, anything we could wind up into a round object. I always had to watch out for my father while playing. If he caught me or if I was late getting home because of a game, a beating was sure to follow.

"Yeah, I know how to play, but . . ."

"But what?"

"Uh," I stammered. My mouth planned to say, "But I have homework to do" or some other lame excuse, but my eyes overruled it. "Are those guys kicking an actual football?" For me, this was right up there with new shoes and my own schoolbooks. A real soccer ball! How could I turn this down?

"Uh, yeah, what did you expect? Come on. Let's play!"

I paused for a moment. The part of my brain that stayed on high alert at all times told me to stay put. *Why are you asking me? What do you really want? Do you want to get me on the field so I drop my guard only for someone to attack me? How can I be safe on that field?* But my love for soccer and the chance to kick a real soccer ball for the first time won out. "All right," I called and chased after him toward the field. "Which team am I on?"

"Mine," he said, and the game began. It did not take long for the ball to come to me. I passed it forward to another boy who was breaking toward the goal. The moment the ball touched my bare foot, a feeling of pure joy washed over me. For just a second, I was a little boy in my home village, playing ball with my friends. But just as quickly, I remembered my father and the beatings he gave me for having fun. I spun around, looking every direction for him. But of course he wasn't there, only boys running around, smiling, laughing, playing a game.

The next time someone asked me to play soccer I hesitated but gave in faster than the first time. I still found myself turning around in panic every ten seconds or so, but the more I played, the easier I found it to relax and have fun. I stopped worrying about being safe and focused on playing the game with boys who were becoming my friends. I also discovered I was pretty good at soccer, which made playing even more fun.

When my first soccer game ended, all of the other guys headed straight for the showers. *I probably should too*, I thought. I'd been at Katweha long enough that my nose blindness to myself had worn off. I stripped off my dirty clothes, stepped under the showerhead, and turned the knob on the wall. *No! This isn't possible. How can so much water come out of the wall all at once?* I thought as cold water poured down on me. (We did not have hot water at Katweha, but you cannot miss what you have never had.) All my life water had been scarce, but this was like something out of science fiction. Unlimited water at the turn of a knob. *No way! But is it unlimited? Hurry up and get the job done before it runs out!* To this day, I still take very fast showers. I guess some habits are hard to break.

A New Hunger

Soccer and friends and showers were nice, but I stayed at Katweha School for the food. I was always the first one in line for breakfast, lunch, and dinner. Many times I went back for seconds and even thirds. *But how long can this last?* I started to ask myself. I knew everything in the world operated on a reward system, so this school had to as well. Up until now, my behavior had not been exemplary. I'd started lots of fights and had yet to go into a classroom. I probably needed to change that soon if I wanted to keep the food train going. I knew I could stop fighting. All I had to do was stop throwing the first punch. But going inside a small classroom filled with other kids? As a street kid, I lived outside every day with no walls, no ceilings, no doors. I went where I wanted and did what I wanted. Going into a small room felt suffocating. Just thinking about it made my heart race.

But I had to go into the classroom or end up back on the streets. *Come on, Peter*, I told myself, *you survived your father and the streets of Kampala. How hard can a classroom be?* I had this conversation with myself over and over until one day I forced myself through the door of the long classroom building. After a couple of steps down the hallway, the walls moved even closer to me. My chest heaved. I could barely breathe. I found my room for my first period class. I think it might have been math. I took a deep breath, pushed myself into the room, and started looking for a place to sit. I found an empty spot next to a student I knew. "Do you mind if I sit here?" I asked.

"No," he said. "Have a seat."

I sat down and tried to get my bearings. Maybe twenty-five or thirty students, boys and girls, filled the room. Some I recognized. Others I did not. I closed my eyes for a minute and tried to catch my breath. I wasn't nervous about being with the other students. Even though I believed they were all on a higher level above me in every way, I have never really cared what anyone else thinks of me. *But this room . . .* I felt my heart racing. How was I supposed to sit in a space so small for the next hour? *I can't do it . . . but I have to.*

Eventually, the teacher came in and class began, which helped take my mind off the fact that I was about to suffocate. Five years without attending school left me behind the other students, but in this class I was able to keep up with the lesson. The teacher paused and asked a question. I thought for a moment. I knew the answer. I raised my hand. She looked right at me. "Peter, do you have the answer to this one for us?"

"Yes," I said, and then I answered the question.

"That's right," she said. "Great job, Peter. Well done."

Great job? No one had ever complimented me for anything in my entire life. *Well done? Whoa. Let's do this again! You thought that answer was cool. Just wait and I'll show you what I can really do.*

From that moment, I had a new motivation to do well in school. I started studying, not to become a better student but to hear words of affirmation from my teachers. I cannot say I craved positive affirmation as much as I desired food, but it was a close second. I had one big problem: I was not at grade level in any of my subjects. When I first arrived, I didn't care about lessons as long as they fed me. But now I did care. The only question was, How was I going to catch up?

I've always had to be resourceful, so I came up with a plan. When other students went off to play soccer, I volunteered to sit out the game and watch over everyone's bags. I knew these guys who had been at the school a lot longer than I had notebooks filled with notes from their classes, notes I didn't have because I hadn't been there. While they played, I studied their notes to try to catch up. The richer kids also had better books, and I helped myself to those as well. Everyone at Katweha loved soccer, which gave me a lot of time to study. The more I studied, the better I did in class and the more praise I earned, which spurred me to study even harder. Before long, a few of my friends gave me their books to read . . . in exchange for doing their homework for them!

My work paid off—but not exactly how I had hoped. The better I did in my classes, the more teachers expected from me, especially my math teacher. Honestly, once I caught up with my friends academically, I didn't have to put in any extra work to dazzle my teachers in class. That's when I learned about tests and grades.

Course grades were not a big deal to me because I had trouble thinking beyond the day in front of me. That's why I did not think much about my math teacher announcing we had a test the next day. Some of the guys with whom I played soccer skirted by with Cs. "As long as we pass the class, what else matters?" they said. *Exactly*, I thought. If I did as well as everyone else, who could complain? Instead of reading while everyone else played soccer, I joined in the game. I knew the material well enough to get by without studying.

I took the test. I knew most of the material, not all, but enough. When I got my paper back, I saw that I had received a C. *Okay. No big deal*, I thought. However, my grade was a big deal to my teacher. "Peter," he said after he handed me my paper, "you are too good of a student to get a C. You are an A student when you do your best. There's no excuse for doing anything less."

Wait. What? I thought. *You expect me to do well every time?* That seemed incredibly harsh, but the more I thought about what he said, the more I realized that he had paid me the greatest compliment of all. Every week he saw me do better and better, and now he was pushing me to do better still. "Peter, look how far you've come," he said to me. "You've already overcome so much. Are you telling me that you can't go any further? I know better than that."

You do? I didn't know that about myself because no one had ever cared enough to call me out and hold me to a high standard. My math teacher and one other teacher stayed on me, pressing me to stay focused and have higher expectations for myself. Looking back, those two made me understand that having potential means nothing if you do not push yourself to do your best.

Dreams

I was playing cards with some of the guys from my dorm when one of them said he had to leave after that hand because he had a biology test coming up. "When is it?" I asked.

"Next week."

"Then why do you need to study now?"

"I have to ace all my bio classes if I ever hope to get into medical school."

I shook my head in disbelief. "Huh?"

"Yeah, I want to be a doctor," he said.

Now my head was really spinning. I knew doctors existed. On the streets of Kampala, one of the street kids in my group got really sick and we found a way to get him to a doctor. But I had never imagined meeting a fifteen-year-old kid who talked about becoming one. Doctors did not come from people like us.

Yet here at Katweha, my friends talked about becoming doctors and engineers and teachers and lawyers and all sorts of professions. They had actual dreams about the future. More than that, those dreams caused them to act in ways I thought were crazy. After spending all day in class, they'd go back to the dorms and study for hours and hours. I was flabbergasted and asked, "Why? Why do you waste your time reviewing your class notes? Are they going to pay you for doing this after you die? Is there some kind of reward I don't know about?"

As it turns out, there was. My friend Andrew explained that the more work I did in school, the better chance I had of attaining my dream job. "What dream job?" I replied.

"Isn't there something you want to do someday?" he asked.

"Not be hungry," I said.

"Come on, Peter. You have to have a bigger dream than that."

I came from a village of farmers where *the* most educated adult had completed only twelfth grade. Even my father had finished only eighth grade. For me, I attended school to survive. Food remained the *only* thing that mattered to me. If my belly was full for the day, I was content. But now Andrew was talking about a world where there was more to life than simply today.

"Do you have a dream job?" I asked.

"Of course," he said, "I'm planning on running my dad's business."

"Wow," was all I could say. The more I hung out with Andrew and other dreamers, the more I started to wonder if I might dare to dream. But I needed something bigger than a dream job. More than anything, I needed to overcome my past. My dream was to feel a sense of human acceptance, to know I could make it in life, and to feel like I belonged. Having a dream job was still many steps beyond achieving the basics of life.

So This Is What the Future Looks Like

All my life I lived in fear of becoming my father. Unfortunately, every man I had ever been around was just like him. The men in my village carried themselves with the same sense of privilege, the same arrogance that said they could do whatever they wanted to whomever they wanted because it was their right as a man. They could do whatever they wanted in their everyday lives. The men in my aunt's neighborhood were more of the same, as were the shop owners and most of the men who came through the bus station in Kampala. I didn't want to be like them, but I did not know any other kind of man existed until James invited me to his home one Sunday to eat dinner with his family.

When James first dropped me off at the school, he promised to come back to check on me. He kept his word. Every week he visited, sometimes by himself and other times with his oldest son or his daughter or both. During our visits, he asked me the kind of questions normal parents ask their children: How is school? How are you adjusting to living here? Have you made any friends? Do you need anything? I always gave him the answers I thought he wanted to hear: "School is great. My classes are wonderful. I have lots of friends. I do not need anything." I did not see this as lying as much as self-preservation. Why tell him about the fights or how I felt like I could not breathe every time I walked into a classroom?

About three months after I arrived at Katweha, James came by for his regular weekly visit. He asked the same kind of questions, and I gave my usual answers. But then James said something that surprised me. "This Sunday I will come by and pick you up so you can go to church with me and afterward we will have lunch with my family. How does that sound?"

Alarm bells went off in my head telling me he had to have some ulterior motive. *Was he going to take me away from the school and throw me back on the streets? Was this his way of getting me outside the gate so I could never come back?* As distrusting as I was, I heard myself say, "Sure. Absolutely. That sounds good."

That Sunday James arrived in his Land Cruiser. A couple of his kids were with him. *Okay, this is a good sign,* I told myself. A little while later we pulled into a church parking lot. "Hey, James. Good to see you," a white man called out. *Wait. What? There are white people in this church? Okay, what is this place?*

I followed James and his kids to the front doors. "There's Martha," he said as his wife and the rest of their children came to meet us. "Where did you park?" James asked her. *Where did she park? That means they have two cars? No one has two cars!*

I was still trying to wrap my head around the whole idea of one family owning two cars when Martha said, "Peter, I'm so glad you joined us today." I had not seen her in a very long time, not since I had last helped her at the marketplace. I was taken aback by this. I was not used to people being glad to see me.

"Thanks for having me," I said.

We went inside. The service started. Every word was in English. The announcements were in English. The songs were in English. The sermon was in English. I looked around. Everyone understood everything being said. *This must be a very educated group of people,* I thought.

The service ended, and we headed toward James's house. I had no idea where he lived. When we pulled into his neighborhood, I still did not know where we were, but I thought we had to be in the richest part of Kampala, perhaps the richest part of Uganda. Looking back, I realize they were essentially American middle class,* but compared to the places I had lived, they were as wealthy as Bill Gates. James pulled up to a large gate, honked his horn, and a policeman opened the gate for him. *Wow. Where am I? What just happened? He lives behind a gate and the police are here to serve him? This must be some house!*

The house itself was large with a tile roof. A green lawn with trees and flowers surrounded the area. Inside, everything was clean, with bright colors on the walls and nice chairs and sofas. The smell of lunch cooking was enchanting. The cook came out and said everything was almost ready. I could not believe they had a cook. They also had a couple of maids working for them. I was overwhelmed and in awe because of the abundance that surrounded me. I felt as if I were at a state dinner with the president. There was more than enough of everything.

But it wasn't the house or the yard or the furnishings or the servants that made an impression on me. Instead, it was James's family. His children all smiled and laughed and played, and James and Martha smiled and laughed with them. I flashed back to my house and my father. My siblings and I stayed clear of my father to keep from setting him off. And he was always yelling, hitting, and cursing. Watching James and Martha and their family, all I could think was, *I am not in Nyabikoni anymore.* In James I saw a man act with gentleness and kindness toward his wife and children. I saw a man treat those working for him with respect. I saw a man

---

*In Uganda, a gated community is not a sign of wealth. The gates are for security. In the same way, everyone feels the need to give back to their neighbors, which is why most people with steady jobs hire cooks and maids as a way of helping those in extreme poverty.

unlike any man I had ever encountered. James and Martha had me back to their home nearly every Sunday after this. Every time I was with them I witnessed the same dynamic.

Watching James's actions stirred up something inside me; I did not have words to describe it. He gave me hope. He showed me I wasn't doomed to repeat the mistakes of my father and his father before him and most every man I had ever seen. I had a choice. I could choose to be like my father, or I could be like James. *This could be my future*, I started to believe.

When it came time to eat, James called me into the dining room with the rest of the family. "Peter, sit over here," he said.

I hesitated.

"Peter, come on over and sit next to me," he said.

I looked around the room. Everyone was waiting for me to sit down. More than that, the look on every face told me I was welcome here. I was no longer an outcast. I had a seat at the table. They told me I belonged.

Embracing the New

I wish I could end this chapter with that last sentence. I wish I could say my life made a dramatic turn at James and Martha's table and I never looked back. But that is not true. I caught a glimpse of a future that I could imagine becoming a reality, which gave me hope, but for hope to take root within a heart, a person must take another step. I had to stop seeing myself through the lens of my past.

When James invited me to his home, I felt like I didn't belong. I wondered why he wanted to share a meal with a street kid who had planned to rob him the first time I had seen him. That's how I still saw myself, but James did not see me that way. Later that day, when he took me back to the school, James told me he thought I was very brave to have come through all I had endured in the past. *Brave?* I did not think of myself as brave, but James did. He did not see me for who I once was but for who I was now.

I believe this is the most difficult step we can take as we try to move beyond our past, and all of us have a past. All of us have been hurt by someone we love. All of us have failed and let people down when they needed us. All of us have stories in our past that we never want anyone to know. When we let our past define us, we shrink back because we feel like we do not fit in or we somehow are not good enough when we have the chance to move forward. I've lived this. When the boys at Katweha first asked me to play soccer, I wondered why they wanted some dirty street kid to join their game. They didn't see me as a street kid. They saw me as a classmate and a friend. Once I saw myself as they saw me, a wall came down that had locked me into a life of hopelessness.

This is a step we all must take, the first step on the journey away from letting our past define us and toward letting it refine us for a greater life in the future.

seven

Normal Redefined

Six months after I arrived at Katweha, I discovered the biggest downside to living at a boarding school: school terms end. My friends could not wait for school to let out. On the soccer field and during our card games, all I heard was, "I'm ready to get home," and "I won't miss the food here. I'm ready for my mom's cooking," and "All I want to do is hang out with my friends." The conversation inevitably came back around to me. "Hey, Peter, what are you going to do during the break?"

My answer never changed. "Ah, you know, whatever." I did not dare tell them the truth: I had nowhere to go. It wasn't like I could go back to sleeping next to the garbage heap at the bus station for two months. I had changed too much in the past six months to survive there. Catching a bus back to Nyabikoni and moving in with my parents never occurred to me. I left home for a reason, and that reason had not changed.

Rather than panic, I did what I had done my entire life: I surveyed the situation around me and looked for options.

There had to be a way for me to convince the school to let me stay right where I was. I had no money to pay rent for two months, but the streets taught me I did not need money to get what I needed to survive.

One day I struck up a conversation with one of the gardeners. "When the school shuts down at the end of the term, who takes care of the grounds?" I asked.

"We do," he answered. "That's when we do most of our work. After all you students leave, we get to work planting and painting and taking care of all the other projects we can't do when you are here."

That's all I needed to hear. I approached the headmaster and asked if I could work on campus during the break in exchange for room and board. I told him I was willing to work anywhere and do whatever they needed me to do. "We always need good workers, and there's always a lot of work to be done," he replied. "But our budget is pretty tight. I don't think we can pay you much beyond letting you live here." I didn't care. Knowing I had a place to stay and food to eat was more than enough payment for me.

A Surprising Option

A few weeks before the end of the term, James came to take me to church and have lunch with his family. On the drive, he turned to me and said, "The school term will end soon."

"Yes, I know," I replied. "My teachers have started getting us ready for our final exams."

"That's good," he said. "The school told me you've done really well this term." I was happy he knew how much I'd grown and accomplished. I wanted him to know his efforts in getting me to school had paid off. "So when the term ends," he continued, "and the school closes for break, my wife and I want you to come stay with us."

"Really?" I said, but inside my mind wondered, *Did he just say what I thought he said?* I had spent many Sunday afternoons with James and Martha and their children, but living with them? Did he remember where I came from?

"Yes. Of course," James said, as if my coming to live with his family for two months was the most natural thing in the world. It wasn't to me. I had changed a lot since I had arrived at Katweha. When I got in his car, James didn't have to roll down the windows because of my smell. I stopped getting into fights with other students, and my grades were good. I had even begun to think beyond the moment and dream about the future. But, deep down, I was still that street kid who had trouble trusting anyone, which made me wonder why anyone would trust me. *Good thing he doesn't know I planned to rob him blind when I first met him*, I thought to myself.

"So, what do you say?" James asked.

He wants me to live in his house. That means he must see me as more than a kid he's helped. It's almost like he sees me as family. Whoa. Family. Me. Really? How can I say no to this? "Yes, that sounds wonderful."

"Great. I'll let Martha and the kids know. They'll be excited."

"So am I," I said in one of the greatest understatements of my life. I was beyond excited. The thought of becoming more a part of this family filled me with exuberance, wonder, disbelief, and joy. I could hardly sit still.

But then I went back to the dorm later that night and started thinking.

NOW I AM KNOWN

And thinking.

And thinking.

I come from a culture that lives for worst-case scenarios, and that's exactly where my mind went. The more I thought about going to live with James and his family, the more questions filled my mind. *What if I break something? What if I break a rule I don't know about? What if I say something offensive? What if . . . ? What if . . . ? What if . . . ?*

And then came the biggest worst-case scenario of them all: *If you move in with them, how long will it take them to figure out you don't belong in their home?* I could hear my father's words ringing in my ears: You don't belong with people like them because you don't belong anywhere. They're rich. You're poor. They have everything. You have nothing. What could they possibly see in a loser like you? James is somebody. You are a nobody, and you will always be a nobody. Nobody wants you. Nobody loves you. Why should this family be any different?

I looked up to James so much that I did not want to let him down. I felt honored that he wanted me to live with him, but I knew the voices in my head were right. I would find a way to mess this up. It wouldn't take long for James and Martha to figure out a street kid did not belong in a house filled with nice things. But that wasn't the worst of it. James was the only person on earth who actually cared about me. When he came to his senses and kicked me out of his house because I broke too many rules, there was no way he would continue to support me at Katweha. And when I could not return to Katweha School, I would have to go back to the streets. And when I went back to living on the streets, not only would I be hungry every day, but I would also have no chance at the future I had just started allowing my mind to imagine. And without a future, I might as well be dead. When I first stepped off the bus in Kampala at age ten, I had nothing left to lose. Now I had everything to lose. My mind fixated on one thought: *What do I have to do to keep from blowing this?*

Neither James nor his wife nor any of his children ever did anything to make me think I had to earn their kindness. My doubts and fears were completely self-inflicted, but that didn't make them any less real for me. I believed the world operated on a system in which everything came at a price. Nothing is ever free, not even kindness. *What will happen to me when I can't live up to their expectations?*

Fish Out of Water

On the day I moved in, James had me share a room with his son Aaron. "This is going to be great," Aaron said when I started unpacking. I was excited too. Aaron was one of the two kids in the car the second time I had seen James in the marketplace. Once I started coming to their house on Sunday afternoons, the two of us became good friends. The two of us hung out the rest of the day, and I almost forgot how out of place I was. And then it came time to go to bed. Bed was no problem. The bedtime "routine" was a new and foreign concept to me.

I changed into my pajamas and started to get into bed when Aaron asked, "Aren't you going to brush your teeth?"

"Do I need to?" I asked.

He laughed. "Uh, yeah."

Now this presented a problem. I was inside, which meant I could not break a stick off a tree. And there wasn't a fire anywhere nearby where I could grab some charcoal and rub it into the stick and then use it to clean my teeth. That's the only kind of teeth brushing I'd ever seen.

When I hesitated, Aaron said, "If you don't have your toothbrush with you, we have some extras." He pulled one out of a drawer and handed it to me. It was the first toothbrush I had ever held. "Here's the toothpaste," he said, handing me the tube.

I stood there, toothbrush in one hand, toothpaste in the other, and I had no idea what to do. I tried to play it cool and act like I had brushed my teeth thousands of times. I mean, who doesn't know how to brush their teeth? The answer was, me! I was smart enough to know the bristle end of the brush went in my mouth, but they didn't look like they'd hold up if I crammed this toothpaste into them and worked it like I worked a stick and charcoal. Eventually, I figured out what to do, but the whole thing made me feel very uncomfortable and very self-conscious.

A few days later, I noticed a wonderful smell coming from the kitchen. "That smells really good," I said to Martha. "I can't wait to eat it."

She laughed. "This is for the dogs."

I nearly fell over. "For the dogs?"

"They need to eat too," she said.

I walked out of the kitchen in complete shock. I could not comprehend making special food for dogs. I was terrified of dogs when I was a small child. When I lived on the streets, we had dogs that hung out with us and I got used to them. Since we were all strays, the stray dogs felt like part of our family. Not James's dogs. They belonged to the security team for protection. *And they cook special food for these scary beasts.* It hadn't been that long since I would have done anything to eat what these dogs ate. *Wow, this family lives a different life.* Our two worlds could not have been farther apart in more ways than one.

One evening James came to me. "We have an event we need to attend. Do you think you will be fine here by yourself?"

"Sure, of course," I said. I knew I would be fine because I didn't plan on doing or touching anything except perhaps a book until the family returned.

"We won't be gone long. Maybe a couple of hours."

I thought I could handle a couple of hours by myself in this nice house without messing anything up. However, after James and the family left, I could not relax sitting in the living room by myself, not with so many nice things around me that I might break. I finally got up to go back to my room. However, on my way out of the room, I brushed up against the wall. Suddenly, all the lights went out. I panicked. What had I done? I moved away from the wall, but the lights did not come back on. I walked to the other side of the room. The house stayed dark. I wondered if maybe the power had gone off for the entire area. I looked out the window to see if other houses had also gone dark. Lights were shining everywhere. I knew I was done for. I had broken something that I had no idea how to fix. As soon as the family came home, they'd see a dark house and know it was all my fault.

Well, I told myself, *it was nice while it lasted.* I went to my room and stuffed all my clothes into my bags. Then I returned to the front room, sat next to the door with my bags, and waited for the inevitable.

An hour or two later, I heard the gate open and the car pull into the driveway. I took a deep breath and prepared myself for the worst. Voices talked and laughed as the family walked up the front sidewalk. The door opened. All at once, to my great surprise, the lights came on. James looked at me sitting on the floor with my bags. "Is everything okay, Peter? You look like you are about to leave."

I looked around the bright room, confused and embarrassed. "I thought I . . . uh . . . I thought I had broken something," I said.

"What?" James asked.

"The electricity. When I leaned against the wall, all the lights went out. I thought I did something to make them stop working."

James smiled and his kids snickered. "You must have hit the light switch, that's all."

"The what?" I asked. I had never used a light switch. We didn't have electricity in our tiny hut in my village. At school, either the lights were on a timer or one of the dorm captains turned them on in the morning and off at night. I didn't know how they worked. I didn't need to know—until now.

"Let me show you," James said. He motioned me to the wall and demonstrated how to flip the switch up to make the lights come on and down to make them go off. I felt a little stupid for not knowing something so basic, but you cannot know what you've never been shown. James was filled with grace. "You know, Peter, just in case, let me take you around the house and make sure you know how to operate anything else that may be unfamiliar to you."

I went from embarrassed to shocked. If this had been my father and not James, at best I would have endured a torment of profanity pointing out how stupid I was. More likely, the flood of profanity would have included slaps to my head or worse. My father did not explain things. He yelled instructions in anger and followed up with a beating if I didn't do things exactly how he wanted. If I had done this in my father's house, I wouldn't have waited for him to come home. I would have gotten as far away from him as I could before his wrath came down on me.

Paradigm Shift

The light switch episode was only a prelude to what was to come. Living with James and Martha showed me what a family could be. No one yelled in this family. Martha did not cower in fear whenever James came home, and their children never hid from their father, afraid of what mood he might be in. They had disagreements, just like any other family, but the parents actually talked with their children. The biggest shock to me came when I watched James apologize to one of his children when he was in the wrong. I hoped James did not notice my eyes nearly jumping out of my head as he did this. My father had never admitted wrong to me or my mother or anyone in all my life. Instead of apologizing, he yelled that much louder. I saw a completely different dynamic in the home of James and Martha, one that resonated deep inside me because it was love, something I'd always longed for but had experienced only from my mom. This was the atmosphere in which I had always wanted to live, but I had long ago given up the idea that a place like this even existed.

Back home, I never ate with my father, but here, the family shared meals together. They talked about what was going on in their lives, shared about friends, plans, and dreams about what they hoped to do. James and Martha asked their children real questions; the adults listened as their children replied. The family liked being together. They even sat down and watched television together. The first time I joined in I was thrilled. I had seen a television through a store window but had never actually watched one. I had never been part of a family event like this either. Today, as a father myself who has lived in America for over twenty years, I find it amusing and sad that something so basic struck me as so unique. The television. Sitting in a living room with family. A calm family. All of it was a novelty to me as a teenager. All of it represented a family functioning as a family should. Even today, I do not take the simple contentment of a peaceful living room shared with family for granted.

I think the thing that may have resonated most strongly with me was how invested James and Martha were in helping their children succeed. The children all went to a different school than the one I attended. Rather than live at a boarding school, they lived at home and the parents drove them to school. This may seem very, very ordinary to most people, and today I log many miles driving my children back and forth to school, but as a young Ugandan teenager, for me this was like spotting the Loch Ness Monster. I kept thinking, *Wait? Parents like this actually exist?* In all the years I lived with twenty-five throwaway kids like me, no one ever came looking for us. No one cared where we were or what time it was. I lived so long in that shadow that I believed my experience was the norm, and I was unaware that there was a bigger world beyond war-torn Uganda. Now I realize some people did care. Some parents were invested in their children. Love actually existed, and in James's home, I not only saw it but also experienced it for myself.

A few weeks after I went to live with James and Martha, James told me they were going on a trip related to his work. "We will be gone for a couple of days. I'd like for you to house sit for us while we're gone."

Are. You. Crazy?! This house was full of nice things. It wasn't like years had passed since I had survived on the streets by taking whatever I needed, with or without permission. I had already made a mental list of all the stuff that I could make disappear in the blink of an eye. I couldn't help myself. I'd lived that way for so long that I could not just turn it off. They really wanted to trust me with all this? I didn't know if I could trust myself.

I did not say any of this. Instead, I looked James in the eye and said, "Are you sure about this?"

"Yes. I'll also leave you some money just in case you want to go get something to eat or if you need anything while we are gone."

Now I had heard everything. He wanted to entrust his nice house and everything in it to a thief boy like me, and now he was going to give me money to boot? "Yeah. I will be happy to do it for you," I said.

I never left the house while they were gone. I was afraid that if I left the gate and went down the street somewhere, someone might break in and steal something and I'd be blamed. On top of that, they left me food in the house. I put that money in my pocket!

There's Always a "But"

Even with James's trust in me, I could not relax. In my mind, I still had to earn the privilege of living with this family.

When it came time to eat, I always held back and did not sit down until everyone else was seated. As soon as the meal was over, I jumped up and started clearing the table and washing dishes rather than joining the rest of the family relaxing in the living room. The moment I climbed out of bed in the morning, I made my bed. I kept my clothes neatly folded and put away. I never left so much as a sock lying on the floor. I never questioned James's and Martha's authority. I never talked back or disobeyed. On Sundays, I was the first one in the car, ready to go to church. When other kids experimented with cigarettes or alcohol or let a curse word slip out, I never did. Never. I did everything I could to live up to James's and Martha's expectations, even the expectations I made up in my head.

My trying to be a perfect kid created tension with Aaron and Anna and the rest of the kids in the family. My efforts for perfection came across like I was trying to make them look bad when they acted like normal kids. My behavior also hurt my relationship with James and Martha. I came across as guarded and ungrateful. Unfortunately, my situation is not unique when it comes to children entering a home through foster care or adoption. Love may try to conquer all, but people are still people. I believed that no matter how fond James may have been of me, in the end, when push came to shove between his biological children and me, I would always come in last.

Once the break was over, I moved back to Katweha School. I still went to church with James and his family and had lunch at their house each Sunday, but when the next break rolled around, I stayed at school and worked. I told James I wanted to do better at school and improve my grades. In reality, I did not feel like I was good enough to live with James's family. I made their love conditional. I told myself I had to work for it. And in my mind, I never worked hard enough. While I spent some weekends with them, I believed that if I stayed for more than a night or two, the entire arrangement might well come crashing down.

I've never completely gotten over these fears. All through my life, I have struggled in relationships because I have always felt that love is something I must work to receive. If I have to earn love, I can never relax and enjoy it. What I do today to earn someone's love may not be enough tomorrow or the next day. I think that is why I have never married. I have always worked so hard for love that even when I am in a safe place with someone who wants the best for me, I still feel like I must be on my toes. I never thought I could find someone who would love me for me, just as I am. I dated many girls when I was younger. I may have even been in love a few times, but the old fears always came roaring back. Unless they had lived through a similar trauma, I believed there was no way they could ever really understand why I am who I am. That is why, ultimately, I've battled the thought that it is best never to marry rather than inflict my brokenness on someone else.

However, I also believe my experiences growing up have uniquely shaped me to be a father to children who have lived through their own trauma. That is why I look back at my early life—running away from home, living on the streets, navigating relationships with James and his family—and see so much good. I wouldn't change a thing because all of what I've lived through brought me to a place where I can offer vulnerable children what James offered me. My entire life hinges on receiving undeserved kindness, and I want to give what I thought I could never deserve: love without strings. How could I not do the same for children who share a similar experience with me? Honestly, James's family gave me that love. They are the reason I am able to parent my kids with gentleness and kindness today. James and Martha expressed love and modeled it over and over and over—until I got it. They persisted in love.

eight

Home

I missed my mom. I thought about her every day. I wanted to see her, but I didn't know if I could. It wasn't just my father keeping me from going back to see her. My mom was pregnant the night I left home. I found out through a relative that she had a miscarriage. I knew I was to blame. When I didn't come home that night, she probably thought I was dead. The shock of losing one child had to have caused her to lose another. I didn't know how I could face her after inflicting so much pain on her.

I knew I could never make amends for her pain, but I thought that perhaps I could still show my mom how much I loved her and how sorry I was for what I had done to her. About three or four months after I started at Katweha, I outgrew the first set of clothes they gave me. Immediately, I thought about my brothers back home. My mother struggled to buy clothes for us when I lived at home. If I could pass along my clothes to my brothers, I might lift a little of that burden from her. I also had several notebooks of class notes I no longer needed but that I knew might help my younger siblings in their school. The school in Nyabikoni did not compare to Katweha. My notes could give my brothers and sister an advantage. But I couldn't just send items for my siblings. I had to scrape together money for items that I wanted to send to my mom. I knew just what to get her.

I stuffed my old clothes and books into a bag and headed to the marketplace where I had once lived. As soon as I arrived, I heard a familiar voice. "Habi! Is that you?"

More voices followed. "Habi? Where?"

"I think it is him."

"No way."

My old friends surrounded me. "Are you real? Is this really you, Habi?"

"Yeah, it's me," I replied.

"No, this can't be you. Your skin and your hair look so different."

"And your smile. When did you learn to smile, Habi?"

"They must be feeding you real good because you are a lot bigger," someone said, which made everyone laugh.

"Check out those clothes. Man, you are looking good."

"Thanks, guys," I said. "It's good to see you too."

"So you need some help carrying your bags?" another said, which made everyone nearly fall over laughing.

"What are you doing back here, Habi? You aren't here to stay, are you?"

"No," I said. "I came to send some stuff back to my mom in Nyabikoni. Have you heard of anyone headed there today?" At that time in Uganda, we did not have a postal system. Instead, if you wanted to send a package, you went to the bus station, found someone going in that direction, and asked them to deliver your package. The system worked. In Africa, if someone gave their word that they were going to do something for you, they did it. Guaranteed.

"Not yet," one of my friends said, "but you know how it goes around here."

"Yeah, someone will show up," I said.

I hung out with my old friends for a few hours, but it wasn't the same as it used to be. We laughed and talked about old times, but I knew and they knew that I was now the opposite of the kid who used to steal with them. They called me Habi just like they used to, but I could tell they looked at me differently, like I was too good to be with them now. I had the life they all wanted. They weren't jealous of me. Instead, they were really happy that at least one of us had escaped the streets, but there was a wall between us now, one none of us felt comfortable breaking down.

Eventually, I found someone traveling near Nyabikoni. I added some sugar and rice for my mom to the package and sent it on its way. Before I left, one of my old friends took me by the shoulder and said, "Don't forget about us, Habi. When you become somebody, come back and help us."

I laughed to myself about the idea of me becoming somebody, but in comparison to who I had once been, I already was. "You guys know I will," I replied. Sadly, life expectancy for those living on the streets is so short that by the time I graduated from the university, none of my friends were still alive to go back to help. However, when I later discovered some of them had kids before they died, I found sponsors in the United States and Europe for their children.

A few weeks later, I received word that my mother was thrilled to receive my package. Maybe she had forgiven me. There was only one way to find out.

On the Road Again

I worked odd jobs around the school to earn enough money to do something I never thought I would do: go home. Not to live, but to visit. My first school year was about to end, and a couple of my friends lived along the way to Nyabikoni. "You guys mind if I tag along on the bus?" I asked.

"What are you talking about? Tagging along? This will be fun," one of the guys named Ben said. Six years earlier I had hidden on a bus alone. Now I couldn't wait to share this experience with a couple of my buddies.

I woke up early the day of my trip. Today, as an adult, when I travel I dress as comfortably as I can. Not on that trip home. I dressed to send a message to my father. I put on my very best shirt, khaki pants, and my blue and white Converse All Star shoes. Although I hated wearing shoes (and I still do to this day), I had to wear them because only the most wealthy people in Nyabikoni owned even one pair of shoes. I had two. I also packed a bag with more clothes and more books for my brothers and sister. When my dad saw my clothes and my shoes and the gifts I brought for everyone but him, he'd see I had already done more with my life than he ever had with his. *In your face, old man!* I laughed to myself. *In your stupid face. You told me I was a useless piece of garbage who would never amount to anything. Well, look at me now! I've already done more with my life than you ever did with yours, and I am just getting started.* When I left home, I was nothing but a scared little boy cowering in fear, taking his verbal and physical abuse. But that boy was gone. If he pushed me, and I hoped he did, I would not back down. All I could think was, *Bring it, old man. Bring it. You'll be sorry you did.*

Ben stuck his head in my dorm. "You ready? We need to get going."

"You better believe it," I said.

We caught a ride over to the bus station along with many other students headed home. When we got out of the school van, I heard that familiar voice once again. "Habi. You're back. What are you doing here this time?"

"I'm getting on a bus to go see my family."

"Need help with your bags?" my friend said with a laugh.

"No. I don't want my stuff to disappear," I replied, and we both laughed. I glanced over at my friends from school. *If they only knew*, I thought to myself.

"You know we don't do things like that," my old friend said with a smile.

"Yeah, right. Hey, I'll see you later. We have to go find our bus," I said.

"Just make sure you get on it and not under it."

I smiled and waved. Neither of my friends from school said a word. "Our bus is over this way," I said. My friends didn't ask why I was so familiar with this bus station, and I didn't tell them. Some things are better left unsaid.

We found our bus and climbed on board. A feeling of déjà vu came over me. Part of my brain told me to get down on the floor and start cleaning out the trash like I had on hundreds of buses over the years. Instead, we found some seats toward the back, shoved our bags under them, and joked around until the bus finally moved. More students from Katweha got on the bus. I couldn't help thinking about my first bus trip. Back then, every time someone got on the bus I slid further down in my seat. Now, the bus had turned into a Katweha party.

The moment the bus pulled out of the station, I felt like my life had come full circle. Five and a half years earlier, I had hidden out of sight on this bus. I didn't know where it was going, and I didn't care. Now I sat up, talking and laughing with my friends and watching the scenery outside the window change. The noise and chaos of Kampala gave way to smaller towns. We passed through the fishing villages on Lake Victoria. Unlike on my first trip years earlier, I gazed out at the lake and let its beauty wash over me. I enjoyed the sound of all the different languages ringing out from the fishing villages. The lake seemed to stretch out forever. The bus stopped at a village. My friend Ben stood up to get off. Outside a woman yelled, "I see him! I see him!" A few kids jumped up and down. An older woman wiped tears from her eyes. "That's my family," Ben said. He turned to me before he climbed off the bus. "Hey, Peter, see you in a couple of months!" he said with a big smile.

"Enjoy your time with your family."

"Yeah, you too."

See you in a couple of months. I smiled. This was not a one-way trip. I had a life and dreams and a future to get back to. I shook my head. *Wow. Had I really been that ten-year-old boy who had completely given up on life?*

The bus started moving again. Several villages turned to safari as we drove near the gorgeous Lake Mburo National Park. All the animals on the savannah were even more wonderful than I remembered. The safari turned into a slow climb up the mountains. With every stop, more students from Katweha got off until I was the only one left on the bus. My village, tucked away in the far southwestern corner of Uganda, was the end of the line. The bus wound along the switchbacks, climbing higher and higher. *These mountains are so beautiful*, I thought. It was almost like I had never seen them before, and I had never seen them like this: as a young man with a future taking in the sights.

Reunion

After thirteen hours, the bus finally reached Nyabikoni. No one was waiting for me because I had not told anyone I was coming home. I wanted my return to be a surprise. I gathered my bags and found a bike taxi. I had too much stuff to carry and couldn't walk two miles from the station to home. The ride to my house took only ten minutes, but it almost seemed longer than the bus trip. I had been so excited to see everyone and to shove my success in my dad's face, but now my stomach twisted into knots. *What if they don't want to see me?* I wished I could train my mind to stop jumping to worst-case scenarios.

My little brother was the first one to see me coming up the road toward our house. He must have thought he had seen a ghost. He didn't even wave. Instead, he spun around and ran into our house calling for my mom.

Then my mom came outside. She covered her mouth and began to weep. I dropped my stuff and started walking toward her. She ran to me, crying and laughing and smiling all at the same time. When she reached me, she threw her arms around me and hugged me so tightly I could barely breathe. "You're home, you're home, you're home," she said over and over. "I can't believe it's you. Oh, why didn't you tell me you were coming?"

"I wanted it to be a surprise," I said.

My mom laughed and hugged me again. "I am very surprised," she said. My brothers and sister came rushing up next. A million arms hugged me all at once. "Go get the chicken," my mom told one of my brothers. "We will feast tonight to celebrate. Your brother has returned!" For our family, this was like the father of the prodigal son killing the fatted calf. We had meat only once or twice a year. To kill a chicken and cook it for me? I cannot describe how momentous this was.

We moved our celebration into my family's small house. My mother served me tea, then we sat down and everyone asked me a million questions. "How is life? How is school? What is Kampala like?" My mother kept shaking her head in disbelief and staring at me like this sight was too good to be true. One of my brothers pointed at my shoes in disbelief. "Where did you get *those*?"

"I actually have two pairs," I said.

"Two pairs! You must be rich!" I just smiled and shook my head. When I first went to Katweha, I thought all the kids in my school had to be rich based on how they were dressed. Now my brother thought that of me. When you have nothing, even a little looks like great wealth.

I pulled out the clothes I had brought for my brothers and sister. Even though they were my hand-me-downs, my siblings reacted like I had brought them the latest fashion from Paris. Then came the books. I explained what each one was and how important learning was for their future. "I want to help you all go to school," I said with more than a little pride in my voice. "I will make sure you have the money for your tuition." My mother said something about how such an act was too much, but I smiled and told her that I had to do this. To me, this was the best investment I could ever make.

I told my mother about my Kampala family and how they made it possible for me to go to school. "They are wonderful people," I told her. "When I am not in school, I live with them. They treat me like one of their own." I did not mention how James discovered me living on the streets near the bus station or anything else about my first five years in the city. My mother knew about my situation, but she did not bring it up and neither did I.

News of my return spread quickly through our small village. Most of my aunts and uncles and grandparents lived nearby, and they all wanted to see me. My mother beamed with pride as she took me from one house to another. "Peter has returned from Kampala, where he's in school and doing so well," she made sure she told each one. My relatives reacted with awe and joy. "Is this true, Peter? You are in school!"

"Yes," I replied.

They threw their arms in the air in celebration. "You, Peter, you are going to do so much," they said, but there was more to their words. When my mother married my father while pregnant with me, she came as an outcast, one never fully accepted. After I disappeared, she carried the shame of losing me. But now, her oldest son was a high school student in a tribe that had never had anyone go past the eighth grade. I now brought hope to an entire family and an entire village and, by extension, the entire tribe. My mother's shame

NOW I AM KNOWN

had been turned into great respect from our family and our village. I saw the change on her face, which made me very happy. I had given her so much pain. I hoped that perhaps this might make up for it.

Face-to-Face with My Father

We feasted on the chicken that night. My father skipped our celebration to go out drinking. I think he heard I was home, but he went straight to the bar rather than come home to see me. We ate without him, just like we did every meal when I was a boy. To me, the meal tasted better without him.

Long after we had finished eating, I heard my father outside our house arguing with someone. *Some things never change*, I said to myself. Eventually, he stumbled through the front door. My mother stopped him. "Peter has come home, so please, do not argue here. Okay?"

My father sort of nodded his head, then started stumbling toward me. "Hello, Peter," he said.

"Hello."

"How are you?"

"Good," I said.

"Okay," he said before shuffling into the other room and falling onto the bed and going to sleep. The next morning he got up early and left while I was still asleep. I knew what this meant. In Africa, when a man feels great shame, he will go to bed and take his pride with him rather than face what has embarrassed him. My return brought such shame to my dad. That's exactly what I wanted it to do.

My father returned home around five the next evening. Once again, I heard him outside, arguing. I went out and saw he wasn't so much arguing as he was harassing someone, and that someone was my mom! When I was a boy, I was too small to protect my mother, but no more. I stepped in front of my mom and said, "You cannot talk to people that way, and especially not my mother."

My father was taken aback. He stood up straight and narrowed his eyes. "Look at you. You go off to school and come back here and think you are really something. Now you think you have the balls to stand up to me?"

"I sure do," I said. "You want to start something, bring it." I did not shake. I did not show any hint of fear because I was not at all afraid. Years and years of rage left no room for fear. All I wanted was to pay him back for all the pain he'd caused me and my siblings and especially my mother. "Did you hear me? I'm not a little kid anymore. I'm not afraid of you. Go ahead, bring it." By this time, my two younger brothers, who were around twelve and fourteen, had come out of the house and were standing not far behind me.

"I think I'm outnumbered," my father said and turned and walked away to the bar. He never raised his voice to anyone the rest of the time I was there.

A Different Send-Off

Two days after I arrived, I was ready to leave. I never planned to stay long. I packed all my things to return to Kampala. The bus still left in the middle of the night, but this time my entire family, my mother and brothers and sister and grandparents and aunts and uncles and cousins, nearly the entire village, everyone except my father, went with me. That's how we send people off in Africa. When someone leaves, everyone turns out to wish them well. We basically throw everyone a going-away party. In my party, when someone asked where I was going, my mother broke out in a huge smile and said, "He's going back to school."

Once we reached the bus station, it took forever for me to actually get on the bus. Every one of my relatives wanted to tell me goodbye. My uncles shook my hand, and all my aunts hugged me with tears in their eyes. No one left the station until the bus pulled away. I turned and watched them as the bus started down the road. Everyone stood and waved until I lost sight of them. I sat back in my seat and thought, *Mission accomplished. I have restored my mother's pride and taken my father's away.* That was exactly what I had hoped to do. As the bus moved farther from my village, the knowledge that this small town was no longer my home grew and grew. I planned to come back every now and then as a visitor, but my future was beyond the Kabale District. As I went back to school, I was determined to finish well. For the next three years, I worked hard and not only graduated from high school but also passed all the entrance exams to go on to college.

I also made good on my promise to my brothers and sister. I paid their local school tuition, and every one of them not only finished high school but also attended the same university in Kampala from which I graduated—Makerere University. Today, one of my brothers is a university professor in Rwanda. My sister works as an executive assistant for a company in Uganda. My next brother teaches high school in Rwanda, and my youngest brother owns his own tour company in Kigali, Rwanda. All of us now live very different lives than our parents or grandparents or any of our aunts and uncles, something that brings me great joy. As I look at where my siblings and I all are today, I cannot help but marvel that all of this, all of what we have accomplished and everything about our lives today, came as the result of the kindness of a stranger to me. The day James first asked me my name set off a chain of events that transformed not only our lives but also future generations through my children and my nieces and nephews.

James's acts of kindness opened up a new world to me, one that I passed on to my siblings and to my children. The small things James modeled broke the cycle of what I had known. His example is what drives me today. I don't know what the future holds for foster children who come into my life or people I speak with at different events, but I know without a doubt that I can make a difference. Right now— today—is all we have to prove life can be different. The question is, Will we grab hold of this opportunity? Everyone deserves to be seen, heard, and known, and when they are, not only their future can change but the world can change as well.

nine

What Hate Can Do

When I first saw bodies floating down the Kagera River out of Rwanda and into Lake Victoria on the local television station, I knew something horrible was happening in our neighboring country. Every day I watched news reports showing hundreds upon hundreds of mutilated corpses floating down the river. Men. Women. Children. Some had been decapitated. Others were cut open with other body parts missing. The bodies of children . . . I cannot speak of what was done to the bodies of the children. Over the course of three months, tens of thousands of bodies piled up in Lake Victoria and washed up on its shore. When the winds came out of the south and east, you could not escape the smell of death. Villagers along the shore buried corpses as fast as they could, racing against the wild dogs and pigs that fed upon them. Fishermen stopped fishing and instead pulled bodies out of the water. Our government ordered us to boil our water before drinking it and to cook fish from Lake Victoria thoroughly before eating it. Like the dogs and the pigs, fish also fed on the bodies floating in the lake. I have not eaten fish since.

The sight of the bodies in the river and the lake shocked me, but I was not surprised that something bad was happening in Rwanda. Wars and atrocities pretty much defined postcolonial Africa. Those outside have blamed the African people, telling us that we lack the skills to govern ourselves. Nothing could be further from the truth. Colonial governments stirred up hatred along tribal lines, creating conflict even in places where conflict between groups had never existed before. As the old saying goes, divide and conquer. In Rwanda, European colonizers ignited hostility between the Hutus and the Tutsis. The Tutsis were smaller in number, but the Belgians put them in power. Then when Rwanda gained its independence, the Hutus took over. Tutsi rebel groups fled the country. Because my home village sits near the Rwandan border, we saw them. In 1990, the rebels went back to Rwanda to try to regain control of the country, and civil war broke out. A cease-fire was signed in 1993. The fighting may have stopped, but the hatred did not. A few months after the cease-fire was signed, someone shot down an airplane carrying then president Juvenal Habyarimana on April 6, 1994. The Hutus blamed the Tutsis and swore revenge. The Tutsis said the Hutus shot down the plane themselves as an excuse to unleash violence against them. No matter who shot down the plane, bodies started flowing down the Kagera River shortly after.

First Job

I was in the middle of my gap year between high school and college, living with friends or with James and doing odd jobs, when James asked if I was interested in a job with an international child advocacy ministry whose Ugandan operation he led. A full-time job that paid well sounded great. "Sure," I said, "but why me?"

"Your home village, it's near the Rwandan border, right?" he asked.

"Yes," I said, not sure where this was going.

"And you speak Kinyarwanda?"

"Of course," I said.

"I'd like for you to go into Rwanda with us. We have reports of hundreds of thousands of children in refugee camps who have been orphaned by the genocide. We have to get food and medicine to them. I'm sending two trucks. I need someone who speaks the language to handle the logistics and make sure the supplies get exactly where they need to be. You will also be in charge of purchasing whatever you discover we need in the country. Can you do it?" he asked.

Rwanda? Now? I thought. By now, everyone in Uganda knew exactly what had happened across the border. Radical Hutus had used machetes to slaughter Tutsis and any Hutus who didn't go along with them. In addition, HIV positive Hutu militiamen had raped thousands of Tutsi women as a sort of living, breathing biological weapon. When Idi Amin ruled Uganda, he killed between one hundred thousand and half a million people. But under Amin, people simply disappeared. Not in Rwanda. I saw the bodies in the water with my own eyes. Supposedly, the worst of the genocide had ended, but who could know for sure? Why would I want to go there?

Yet I could not say no. How could I turn James down after all he had done for me? And this was no small job he asked me to take. By putting me in charge of the logistics, he placed the success of the operation in my hands. If he trusted me this much, I had to accept. "Okay," I said. "I will do it." This was my first real job with adult responsibilities and included weeks of being away from my familiar surroundings, leading a mission, and working with many other team members.

A few days later, I found myself in the front seat of a semitruck headed toward the Ugandan and Rwandan border. I tried to mentally prepare myself for what was ahead, but my mind had trouble making sense of the numbers we kept hearing. Two hundred thousand dead . . . three hundred thousand . . . five hundred thousand . . . the numbers did not seem real. (Ultimately, the United Nations estimated that at least eight hundred thousand people died over the course of one hundred days.) The sight of corpses in Lake Victoria already haunted me, as did a thought I could not push out of my mind: *Why would those hacking people to death with machetes spare us?* We weren't Hutu or Tutsi or even Rwandan, but that didn't matter. This was a humanitarian mission, but there did not seem to be much humanity in those doing the killing. I could not help but wonder if any of us would get home alive.

Name

My fears jumped to a new level when we arrived at the border. Soldiers motioned for us to stop our trucks. One soldier who appeared to be in charge told us to exit our vehicles and take our passports and other identification papers to the window of a small office off the side of the road. The process went fairly quickly for everyone on our team. They lined up at the window and handed over their passports.

An official looked over each one, turned to a page in the back, stamped it, handed it back, and motioned for the next person to step up.

But I didn't have a passport. I didn't think anything of it when I walked up to the window and handed over my identification papers. Uganda and Rwanda had always had an open border, no passport required. I was born near the border. I saw people move from one side of the border to the other all the time. It was no big deal, and that's what I expected now.

The man glanced over my identification papers, then his eyes jumped up to me. I smiled. He didn't smile back. Instead, he got up and showed my paperwork to another man. A third man came over, and the three started talking among themselves. After a few moments, the first official walked back to the window and said, "We need you to come with us." Before I could ask any questions, a soldier with a gun made it clear that I needed to go right then.

The soldier led me to a door on the side of the building. The official opened it and motioned for me to come inside. The soldier followed me. "Have a seat," the official said. I did exactly as I was told. My heart beat faster, and sweat beaded up on my forehead. I felt like I was in trouble, but I had only just now crossed the border. What could I have done?

The official held my paperwork in front of him. "So, Peter, where were you born?"

"Nyabikoni in Uganda," I said.

"Who do you work for?"

I was surprised by this question. The name of our organization was written on the side of our trucks. I answered him anyway.

"How long have you worked for them?"

"I worked off and on part-time as a translator while I was in school," I said.

"Why did they send you into Rwanda?"

"They needed someone who speaks Kinyarwanda to translate on this trip."

"Where did you learn Kinyarwanda? Have you been to Rwanda before?"

I wondered where this line of questioning was going. "I grew up speaking it in my village in Uganda. Many people there speak it. But no, I have never been to Rwanda before."

"Who do you know in Rwanda?"

"No one."

"Relatives. You must have relatives here in Rwanda," the official said.

For a moment, I wondered why he thought that, and then it hit me: my last name. The culture of our tribe was not to assume the father's last name. When I turned two and my mother was sure I was going to survive and grow, she gave me the Kinyarwanda name Habyarimana, which roughly means "a gift given to me by God." Since most people in Uganda do not speak Kinyarwanda, I constantly heard, "Your name is so long. What does it mean?" However, in Runkiga and Runyakore, two languages also spoken in my village, my last name sounds like the word for vagina. I cannot tell you how many times other kids laughed at me because of my name.

No one at the Rwandan border was laughing now. They stopped me because Habyarimana was also the last name of the president whose plane was shot down, igniting the genocide. He was Hutu. Those killing their neighbors with machetes were Hutu. Now here I was at the border claiming to be Ugandan, but without a government-issued passport, I had no proof. What I did have was the last name of the one in whose name the radical Hutus had started this slaughter. If I were in these officials' place, I might have been suspicious of me as well.

I did my best to explain how I received my last name. They must have believed me because after about an hour of questioning, they let me rejoin my group. On my way out the door, one of the officials said, "You know, you might want to think about changing your name." I smiled and nodded, but inside I was in full-scale panic. *What am I doing here? If others learn my last name, will I make it out of here alive?* No job was worth this. I also thought, *If I get out of here alive, the first thing I am going to do when I get home is get my Ugandan passport!*

No Limits to Hate

After my one-hour delay, our trucks finally started into the interior of Rwanda. We had not traveled far when I noticed a bulldozer pushing dirt into a long trench. Crowds of people stood on either side of the trench, staring down into it, expressionless. I looked closer. This was not a trench but a mass grave holding what looked like to be as many as five thousand bodies. The overwhelming smell of death hung in the air. The truck driver and I just stared and did not say a word. I don't know what I expected to see, but I was not prepared for this.

Our trucks kept moving. All along the road we passed lines of people slowly walking, their eyes staring off into space like they were zombies. They did not look up at us as we passed or jump out of the way when our truck got too close. Other than their legs moving their bodies along, they showed no signs of life. I could not help but wonder which side of the genocide they had been on. Were they in shock over what they had done or in shock because of what had been done to them? And if they were the former, what kept them from turning on us? I felt my heart start to race. I struggled to breathe. *There's no way I will survive this.* I did not dare say the words out loud, as if speaking them guaranteed they would come true, but I could not help thinking them. I knew beyond a shadow of a doubt that this was going to be a one-way trip. The same people who had hacked up their neighbors with machetes would see to that.

A little farther down the road we passed a boarded-up church. The building itself looked fine. "I wonder why they closed down churches? It doesn't look like anyone attacked the building," I said. The driver and I had seen enough burned-out houses to know what it looked like when an attack had taken place.

"Do you really want to know?" the truck driver asked.

"Yeah," I said, not sure if I did or not.

"Some pastors and priests and even nuns invited people to come hide in their churches for refuge. Once the church was full, they called for the Hutu militia, which came in and killed everyone inside," he said. The buildings stood, but the people did not.

"How . . ." I started to ask but stopped myself. I knew how someone could do something so horrific: hate. All around me I saw the evidence of how when hate fills the heart, anything is possible. There are no limits to the evil human beings can unleash upon one another. I had read about things like the

Holocaust in school, but reading about it in a book does not compare to seeing it played out in front of you.

How can people hate this much? I wondered, but then another thought hit me like a brick flying through the truck window. I knew how someone could hate so deeply, because I held on to a hate this deep in my own heart. It was part of the reason why I always found God and religion so unpalatable. I acted the part of a good Christian man. I went to church when I attended Katweha and had continued even after finishing high school. I taught Sunday school classes and volunteered wherever anyone needed me. But I never bought in to the central core of the whole system. I never believed in the idea of forgiving those who had wronged me. I got it when it came to minor offenses. Life went much better for me after I learned to talk through misunderstandings with my friends rather than picking them up and trying to throw them through a window. Yet even that served my best interests. If I had continued to punch my way through every dispute, I would have been kicked out of school and would have had to say goodbye to my three meals a day. I really had no other choice than to forgive.

However, when it came to the one person who had hurt me the most, I refused to consider forgiving him. My father beat me mercilessly until I ran away. He convinced me I did not matter, that I was worthless, that my life was nothing but a burden, and that the best thing I could do for him and everyone else in the world was to lie down and die. I hated him for it. I did not just wish him dead. I wanted to see his life torn down. I wanted to see him live in embarrassment and shame and disgrace, and I wanted him to have to look up at me and see the man he could never hope to be.

I dreamed of success—so that I could shove it in his face just like I did on my first trip home. But even that was not going to be enough. When I lived on the streets, my friends and I used to defecate on the fruits and vegetables of the shopkeepers who crossed us. I dreamed of doing the same on my father's grave. That's how he treated me my whole life. I figured he had it coming. Forgive him? That's ridiculous. Forgiveness only makes you weak and sets you up to be hurt again. I refused to allow my father to ever hurt me again. From now on, I planned to be the one to hurt him every chance I got.

Driving down the road in Rwanda, watching the living dead stagger past us, looking out on burned-out houses and boarded-up churches, I could not help but wonder how different those who had committed these atrocities were from me. Did they feel as justified in acting on their hate as I felt toward my father?

And All Had a Story to Tell

Just outside the first town through which we passed we came to a refugee camp. A guard opened the gate, and we pulled inside. Immediately, hundreds of children surrounded our trucks. I guess kids will always be kids, which made the sight of these big trucks and smiling strangers exciting for everyone. One of the officials told us we were the first people from the outside allowed into the camp. Adults did not live here, only children orphaned by the genocide. They ranged in age from babies to twelve or thirteen. Camps like this had never existed in Rwanda before. Throughout its history, as in most African countries, when a child lost both parents, relatives took them in. But there were no relatives for these children. All had either been killed or fled the country.

As soon as I got out of the truck, I went to work helping unload the sacks of grain we'd brought in for the children. Once the food was unloaded and all the paperwork was signed, I and the rest of our team spread out to interact with the children. I found a spot to sit down, and immediately children flocked to me, but these were not ordinary children. Many were missing arms. Almost all had scars on their arms or legs and heads. For many, the wounds were still fresh, but that did not stop them from wanting to play and to talk to me. They all wanted to talk because every one of them had a story to tell.

"My mother shoved me under the bed and told me to hide there when we heard the bad people come to our house. I saw her fall down on the floor in front of me. She was bleeding really bad. I knew she was dead. . . ."

"My best friend next door, his dad killed my dad with a machete. . . ."

"I saw a man who lived down the street hit my mommy in the head with a hammer. . . ."

"When the bad people came to our house, my mommy and daddy told me to run as fast as I could out into a field and not stop running until I was far away from there. I never saw them again. . . ."

Every time one child told me a story, five more, ten more, spoke up. It was like each one had to verbalize what they had lived through. I guess talking about it was their first step on a long, long journey of healing, if healing was even possible. One story in particular haunts me to this day. A little boy told me how his father killed his mother. "He said he wanted her to die peacefully because he knew the neighbors were gonna come and do really bad things to her and kill her," the boy said. I looked deep into the boy's eyes. *How can he possibly have a life after this?*

The more stories to which I listened, the more I knew that nothing I could do would lessen their pain even a little bit. I kept my mouth shut except to tell them how sorry I was. People who have lived through trauma desperately need someone who cares enough to listen to their stories, just as James and many of my teachers at Katweha did for me. Hurting people need to be heard. They need to know they are not alone. These children who had lost everything needed to know they still mattered. The only way I could do that was by listening to one story after another, even when I thought my heart could not bear hearing another child describe in detail what it was like to watch their mother and father die at the hands of people they once thought of as friends. The stories all sounded so much alike, but for these children, each story was as unique as they were. I hated to leave when it came time to move on to the next camp filled with orphaned children, but I had no choice. Other hungry children were waiting there, children who also needed to be seen and heard and loved.

For five days, we visited refugee camp after refugee camp. Each one was filled with children covered with both physical and emotional scars that came from living through one hundred days of hell. For the first few days, I found myself in a near panic. The more stories of atrocities I heard, the more I wondered what made me and this team so special that we might escape the same fate. If neighbors slaughtered their neighbors, if pastors and priests and nuns turned over their congregations to be killed, why wouldn't they turn on us? My fear and panic drove me to pray, "Please, God, if you will allow me to live and return home, I will be an advocate for these children for the rest of my life." I meant it. I could think of no better way to spend my life than making a difference and speaking up for those who could not be heard.

God took me safely home from Rwanda. And I did what I promised, but not out of guilt that I had to keep a vow I had made in desperation. Looking into the eyes of the young victims of the Rwanda genocide, I discovered my purpose in this life. I thought I had lived through the worst any child could endure, but my experience did not compare to what I saw during my first of many trips to Rwanda. I could not stop wondering how many more children were out there enduring trauma and pain. If I didn't speak up for them, who would?

The Last Hold of the Past

After five days of delivering relief supplies to children's refugee camps, we finally started back north to Uganda. I still held my breath, wondering if a militia group had a roadblock up ahead where they'd drag us out of the trucks, hack us to death, and take our vehicles. Thankfully, we never encountered any problems. We drove back over the roads we came in on. We saw more mass graves, more closed-up churches, more living zombies slowly walking along the roads, but at least we were headed home where we could leave these horrors behind us. I don't think I fully relaxed until we finally crossed into Uganda.

I had a lot of time to think during the drive home. My mind kept running back to the same question that had hit me soon after we had arrived: How different was I from the people who had carried out this genocide? They were motivated by hate. They felt justified in carrying out acts that defy description. *If given the chance, would I do the same to my own father?* I had to admit there were times in my life when the answer was yes. I wanted to see him die. I wanted him to suffer as deeply as he made me suffer.

That's when it hit me. I told myself that I had overcome my past. After all, I had finished high school and had been accepted by Makerere University. I had hopes and dreams for my future. I had already achieved more than anyone in my family, and I was far from satisfied. I planned to do more—much, much more. *Why?* I asked myself. What really motivated me? Was it to reach my dreams, or was it to crush my father? My father had told me I would never amount to anything. I wanted to prove him wrong. But then what? I realized that my hatred for my father and my desire to rub my success in his face only showed how strong my past still had ahold of me. I thought I had moved past who I had once been, but now I realized that it was like I had never left my father's house. I had not grown. My father still had as much control over me as he did when I was a little boy. Hating my father motivated me and defined me. I really did not know who I was apart from it.

Five days in the hell that was postgenocide Rwanda made me realize I had hated long enough. I had to be free of the bitterness before it consumed me, as it had consumed Rwanda's countryside. Perhaps I would never lash out toward my father like one tribe had lashed out against the other in Rwanda, but as long as I held on to my hate and refused to forgive, I was no more alive than the people I saw staggering down the roads or standing next to the mass graves.

During this trip to Rwanda, I realized that forgiveness was what I finally had to experience with my father. The whole idea of forgiveness means releasing another from their debt. With God's help, I turned loose the debt of pain my father owed me. This marked the beginning of my life of faith, and through the lens of faith, I finally saw my father for who he was: a lost man in need of hope, just like I had been.

Not growing up with a loving father impacts me every day, and it can trigger sadness or motivate me toward goodness. But my hope gave way to understanding and forgiveness toward my father. He did not have to change to earn my forgiveness. Instead, I saw that he was who he was. He remained the angry, mean, argumentative person he had always been, but I knew I could not do anything to change that. I simply had to accept him for who he was. Once I saw him in this way, I discovered his words could no longer exact an emotional toll from me. Forgiveness not only set me free from my past but also took away my fear for the future. I could now embrace my past and use it to make a difference in the lives of children.

In the years since my first trip into Rwanda, I have traveled all over the world. I have seen firsthand the destructive power of hate, but I have also seen the healing power of generosity, acceptance, and love. The latter is our only hope. We all have the opportunity to help others, inspire others, and love others from a sincere heart. I've worked hundreds of hours to help impoverished children move into opportunity. My passion for giving kids a chance to be known, be heard, and be seen goes beyond any other dream I've ever had. And spreading that message to adults is equally necessary. I know firsthand that if you don't deal with the hate you experienced as a child, it will continue to influence your future well into adulthood. That's what hate does: it keeps us locked, stuck, and prevents us from the growth we are meant for. But forgiveness can set us free.

The thing I love most about expressing unwavering acceptance is that each person in this chain of hope and love and forgiveness will share, help, or impact another's life in a different manner needed to create community. Each one of us has something unique to share with the world.

One final note about forgiveness. Remember, in our tribe, a family name is not passed down from generation to generation. My last name, Mutabazi, was my father's last name. I took it when I became a United States citizen in 2019. For much of my life, I wanted nothing to do with him, but once I was set free from my anger and hate and truly forgave him, I accepted that I am forever connected to him. He is my father, no matter who he is or what he has done, and I am his son. I embraced my past rather than running from it or resenting it for the rest of my life. Mutabazi is more than a name. It is a reminder of the power of forgiveness. That does not mean I instantly stopped struggling in my relationship with my father. I still struggle at times today, which forces me to renew my decision to forgive every day.

ten

Dream Bigger

I heard my dad had been bragging about me to his drinking buddies. Typing these words twenty-five years later doesn't make them any less strange for me. My father was bragging to all his friends about *me*, the son he told would never amount to anything, the one he called a worthless piece of garbage every day for the first ten years of my life.

I heard about my father's radical change of heart toward me as his son during one of my trips back to Rwanda. Even though I begged God nonstop every day to let me get out of Rwanda alive during my first five-day trip, I still went back . . . more than fifty times within eighteen months! The highway from Kampala to Kigali, Rwanda, ran through my home village. On several of my relief missions to Rwanda, our team spent the night in a hotel near my parents' home. And during one of those stays, a man recognized me outside on the road. "You're Mutabazi's son, aren't you?" he called out.

I was surprised. "Uh, yeah."

"I thought so. I'm friends with your dad, and let me tell you, you're all he ever talks about these days."

"Excuse me?" I replied.

"Every night he never shuts up about you. All he ever talks about is how you're on your way to university."

The man did not have to say which university. In Uganda during the mid-1990s, Makerere University was the only university for an entire nation of over twenty million people. Imagine Florida or New York having a single college or university in the entire state. That's what it was like for us. Makerere was also highly selective about who they accepted. Very few of those who applied actually got in.

"You're sure my father was talking about me?"

"Are you kidding? All I ever hear from him is Peter is going to university. Peter aced all his entrance exams. Peter is so smart. Peter this. Peter that. Peter, Peter, Peter."

My jaw dropped. I thanked the man, turned around, and went back to my hotel room in stunned silence. Six months earlier, I would have marched over to my father's favorite bar, got in his face, and told him he had no right to say anything to anyone about me. I would have told him that I accomplished everything in spite of him, not because of him. But that first trip to Rwanda had changed me, and the change in me became more and more complete with every trip.

By God's grace, anger and hatred toward my father no longer consumed me. Even though my father had not changed at all, I had matured. He was who he was, but I didn't have to suffer because of the misery and behavior he chose to live out. The weight of anger and hate related to my childhood diminished as I realized there was more life ahead of me.

That grace allowed me to say to myself, *Wow, my father is actually proud of me. That's pretty much a miracle.*

But it wasn't just my father who treated me differently. My mother cried when I first told her I had been accepted by Makerere, and then she went out and told all her friends. I expected that. However, I was surprised with the way people in my village treated me while I was there. Old friends from when I was a boy treated me almost like a celebrity. Aunts and uncles who never really accepted my mother or any of her children shook my hand and patted me on the back. "Peter," one of my uncles said with a solemn voice, "when you go to Makerere, you are not alone. Your family, your tribe, all of Nyabikoni goes with you." I understood what he meant. In Nyabikoni, drunks and prostitutes outnumbered people who had attended high school one hundred to one. Very few jobs existed, which left most people no other option but to work small farms that never produced enough for everyone to eat. Starting in the late 1980s, HIV and AIDS swept through our village as they devastated east Africa. Every family lost someone to the virus, and our family was no exception. Many friends with whom I had once played soccer with a ball made out of rolled-up banana leaves died from the virus. Nothing good ever came out of Nyabikoni, and everyone knew it. No one in Nyabikoni dared dream of better days.

And then I was accepted into Makerere University.

I was the first child born in Nyabikoni that I knew of to go to college, which didn't just make my village proud of me. I gave them hope. My academic success changed the expectations for the entire village. Doors now opened. The impossible was possible. My life gave the rest of my family and the rest of my tribe and the rest of my village permission to dream of possibilities rather than give up and give in to fate. My acceptance to Makerere University wasn't just about me and my hopes and dreams for the future. I carried the hopes and dreams of an entire village with me. As this truth slowly dawned on me, all I could think was *DON'T BLOW THIS!* I told you, Ugandans have a knack for fixating on worst-case scenarios.

The next change within myself came when I moved into my dorm at the beginning of my freshman year. Even though I had lived at boarding school, I still felt a little intimidated by the university. Katweha was a small Christian school, and Makerere had well over ten thousand students on campus.

Music blared as I walked down the hall of my dorm looking for my room. Guys hung out in the hallways, talking, laughing, having a good time. Classes hadn't started yet, so everyone was happy and relaxed. "Hey, how ya doin'?" one after another said as I weaved in and out of the crowd. When I found my room, the door was open. I walked inside and saw that my roommate had already moved in. Before I could set my bags down on my bed, a guy came into the room and said, "Hey, you must be Peter. I'm Josh. Looks like we're going to be living together for a while."

"Oh, great, uh, Josh. Yeah, I'm, uh, I'm Peter. Great to meet you."

"Yeah, great to meet you too. I moved in a couple of days ago, so I guess I got a little head start on you. Drop your stuff and come on out in the hall. I want to introduce you to some of my friends," Josh said with a big grin.

"That sounds great." I dropped my stuff and headed out into the party going on in the hallway. I'm not really a shy person, but I suddenly became one, maybe because I have never been much of a celebration guy. I don't even celebrate my own birthday. To be honest, I just wanted to start unpacking my things in my room and get ready for the start of the term. But I did not want to appear antisocial, so I followed Josh over to a group of about ten guys.

"Hey, guys, this is my roommate, Peter," Josh announced. The other guys greeted me like they'd known me all their lives. From the start, I sensed a kind of mutual respect. All of us had worked hard to get here. Academically, every student had to be at the top. No one did us any favors by letting us into Makerere. We all earned admission, which put us on equal footing. I have to say, that felt really good. Not one of these guys knew anything about my background. They didn't know about how I ran to get away from my father at the age of ten. Nor did they know about my years of survival on the streets of Kampala. But the best part was they didn't need to know, and I wasn't going to tell them. To them, I was just another freshman like everyone else. *My past really doesn't define me anymore, only my future.* That thought felt liberating.

A few days later, Josh asked if I wanted to get a drink with him and a couple of the other guys from our floor. I don't drink, but I went anyway just to hang out. On our way to the bar, Josh said, "My friend Semwo will meet us there. He's a good guy. We're in some of the same classes."

"Okay. Cool," I said. The name didn't register when I heard it, but I had to keep my eyes from growing wide when we walked into the bar and I saw who was waiting for us. "Hey, Semwo, this is my roommate, Peter," Josh said.

"Peter, great to meet you."

"Yeah, you too," I said, trying to keep my jaw from dropping and my voice from shaking. Semwo wasn't just another student. His father was the Ugandan prime minister. In the Ugandan system, the president is the head of state, but the prime minister leads the government. In those days, people treated politicians like gods. Past governments conditioned that response from us. Now here I was, hanging out at a bar with the son of the most powerful man in Uganda like this was the most natural thing in the world.

Here's the craziest part: Semwo and I hit it off from the start. He asked about my major and why I chose it, and I asked about his. We talked about what we liked about the university and our future plans. He told me he wanted to return to America, where he had been born and gone to school. Growing up, he spent more time in the States than in Uganda. Many kids from wealthier families split time between Uganda and the US or Great Britain. I did not mention how I spent a huge part of my growing up years living on the streets. I didn't really think it mattered, and it didn't. Over the course of the night, Semwo and I talked about a little bit of everything except our family backgrounds. I didn't ask about his, and he didn't ask about mine because neither mattered. We were just two students far from home, hanging out with our friends. And we did become friends, not just while we attended the university but still to this day.

As I walked back to my dorm room after that first meeting, I could not help but pinch myself. *This is crazy!* I told myself over and over. How can a kid who grew up on the streets hang out with the prime minister's son on completely equal footing? This shouldn't happen, and yet it felt perfectly normal, just like all my college friendships did. I belonged just like everyone else.

Straddling Two Different Worlds

I started my classes, and I did pretty well. Semesters came and went. I continued working part-time for the same relief organization that took me to Rwanda, and I sent money back to Nyabikoni for my siblings' education. On the weekends, I taught a children's Sunday school class and did other volunteer work at the same Baptist church I had attended while at Katweha. The pastor and I became close, which I enjoyed. Church actually meant something to me now that I had stopped going through the motions of being a believer and actually lived the part.

Then I met a girl.

I met Julia at the airport with James. She had come to Kampala to work with children from America and Europe in an international school. He told me her last name sounded like the word *petite*, which of course is the French word for small. But she wasn't small. Her stature surprised me. I had known her about thirty seconds when I said something like, "I expected you to be small." She immediately disliked me and refused to have anything to do with me during the car ride from the airport. I had no idea why, but since I did not think I would see her again, I didn't give it much thought. However, we kept running into each other at events for diplomats, nonprofit leaders, and missionaries. Julia taught the children, while James worked with the parents. Since I worked closely with James, it seemed Julia and I could not avoid each other, although she tried. Whenever she saw me, she went the other way.

The first time this happened I dismissed it as no big deal. However, the more she avoided me and gave me an angry look when I said hello to her, the more I wanted to find out what I had done to offend her. Finally, I stopped her long enough to ask, "Julia, why do you dislike me so much? We don't even know each other."

"Apparently you know me well enough to call me fat," she replied.

"Wait. What? When did I do that, because I never would have said something like that. You are not fat," I said.

"When we first met. You said you expected me to be small."

Then I got it. "No, no, no. It was because of your name, Petitte. In French, it means small or little, so I expected you to be little, like, short. Believe me, it was just your name."

She believed me . . . eventually. *Welcome to the world of American women* was all I could think once I discovered my mistake. I have now lived in the United States for twenty years. I became an American citizen in 2019 and have been a foster dad to three daughters. I still don't understand American women any better today than I did then.

Julia finally forgave me, and we started dating about six months after we first met. Not long after, she asked me to come with her to a party being thrown by the parents of one of her students. The look on my face said no before my mouth could. I have never been one for parties, especially with a crowd of people I don't know.

"Oh, come on, Peter. It will be fun. Besides, I need you there with me. Everyone else there will be married, and I really don't want to go by myself."

I sort of groaned. "Oh, I don't know. Where's the party going to be?"

"The United States Embassy," Julia said.

Honestly, that made me want to go even less, but I agreed so I could support Julia. Because of James's work with an international relief organization, he often had Europeans and Americans in his home. Living with James's family off and on, I spent a lot of time around foreign visitors. But going to the American Embassy was a new level. No longer was I in the background. Every person in the room with children knew Julia from her work with their kids. And she introduced me to everyone as her boyfriend. Most asked the same question: "And what do you do, Peter?"

"I'm a student at Makerere University."

"Oh, I hear that's a good school. What are you studying?"

"Business administration."

"Oh, that's a great field," and the conversations took off from there.

The longer I dated Julia, the more interaction I had with important people from around the world. The Irish ambassador became a friend. I got to know various US Marines at the American Embassy since most were close to my age. Before long, if I did not attend events with Julia, people asked her about me. When I first started at Makerere, my whole world consisted of Uganda and Rwanda and our small spot in the middle of Africa. Dating Julia literally opened up my life to the world. As surprising as it may sound, I felt completely at home mixing with people from all cultures and walks of life. I had an American roommate, worked with Westerners alongside James, and had my surroundings expanded so many times since I first climbed on the bus to run away from home that now finding myself immersed in another foreign environment felt completely natural.

Back to My Passion

Julia and I had been dating awhile when she asked if I liked to run. What kind of question was that? "I don't know," I said. "Not really. If I run, that usually means I'm trying to get away from a wild dog or something that might hurt me."

"Not like that. I mean to run for fun. For exercise."

Wow. Who runs for exercise? Who even exercises? I did not have a car. If I had to go across town, I took a bus, but most of the time I walked everywhere. Everyone in Uganda walked everywhere. Day-to-day life gave me plenty of exercise. I didn't think I needed to run for more. I didn't say any of this. Instead, I simply said, "That's something I've never even thought about doing."

"We should start running. It will be fun. There's a running club nearby where we can go. A lot of people are members." By a lot of people, she of course meant a lot of Americans and Europeans. No Ugandans outside of athletes hoping to go to the Olympics joined a club to run, and I did not plan to go out for the Olympic team.

"I'll try it," I said, which was good enough for her.

My first trip to the running club was every bit as strange as I had imagined. The place had a track filled with white people running around in a very large circle. No one ran to get anywhere. They just ran around and around and around, ending up exactly where they started. *These people are crazy*, I thought but didn't dare share my opinion out loud.

However, I recognized some of the people from my contacts through both James and Julia. One saw me. "Hey, Peter, I didn't know you were a runner."

"Oh, yeah. I've been running my whole life." *From dogs, from fights, to go fetch water, to get away from my dad. Oh yeah, I've always been a runner.*

"Good to see you. Hey, let me introduce you to a friend. Come on, run with us." And that was really all it took for me to become a part of the running club. I did not see any point in running around in circles, but it looked like a good way to socialize. I had friends from school, but most liked going out to bars at night and on weekends. Since I don't drink, and bars bring up bad memories of my father's drunken rages, running was a way to hang out with people.

I kept going back to the running club, sometimes with Julia but more and more by myself. I rarely ran alone. I still didn't see the point in that, but I liked to run with other people.

One Saturday at the club, I got to know Eric. Like most guys everywhere, he asked what I did. When I told him I was a university student, he asked about my major. Then I asked what he did. "I work for the ICRC," he said.

"The what?" I asked.

"Sorry. The International Committee of the Red Cross," he said.

That piqued my interest. I told him about my numerous trips into Rwanda with another relief organization. "That's the kind of work we do," he said. "With the fighting in Sudan and Chad, there's always a lot of work that has to be done."

"So, do you have any jobs available?" I asked. "I've done a lot of work as a translator since I speak Swahili and French along with English and some other tribal languages."

"As a matter of fact, we do," he replied. "But I don't think you'd be interested in what we have available."

"Why not?" I asked.

"We need a nighttime radio operator who can help co-ordinate our trucks and planes as they go in and out of the countries around here. The hours are terrible, and the pay is even worse."

I spent my nights studying. This sounded like a way to get paid while I did it. "I'll take it," I said.

"Really?" My new friend sounded surprised. He shouldn't have been. Jobs were hard to come by in Uganda. Even though I already had one part-time job, it was barely enough to cover my expenses. By the time I sent money home for my siblings, I was really struggling to get by.

More than the money—and my friend was right, it wasn't much—the job appealed to me because it gave me a chance to make a difference. I had been a part of so many relief trips that I knew exactly what the truck drivers and other workers faced. In Rwanda, I also saw the devastation war leaves behind. If I could help make a difference in Sudan and Chad and wherever else the ICRC needed to go, the job would be worth it to me.

Dream Bigger

I kept my overnight, part-time job with the ICRC for the next three years. It turned out to be not just a part-time job but a prelude to my career. I have worked for one international relief agency after another ever since I took that job. I had a lot of friends in college who already had really good jobs when they arrived at Makerere. One worked in the largest British bank in Kampala. Another was an accountant who already owned his own home and car. Another friend came from a family that owned a large chain of grocery stores in Uganda. Hanging out with these guys made me dream big; I finally realized I could have a job like those someday. However, I look back and realize those dreams were too small. Working as a radio operator coordinating relief missions made me a part of something much bigger than myself. I didn't know it then, but without the ICRC experience, I would not be where I am today.

I also would not be where I am today if I had never met Julia. She opened a door for me into a world without boundaries. Our romantic relationship eventually came to an end. I could never get over my fear of becoming like my father, which kept me from getting serious about her or any other girl. After dating for two years, we parted as friends, but by then my path was taking me places I never imagined. And until I started writing this book, I didn't realize that the path started when I hopped in James's car to pick up someone at the airport like I had done a thousand times before.

Before I met Julia, I only dared to dream small, hoping to perhaps carve out a decent living for myself. I think a lot of us dream too small. As I consider my life—James, Katweha, Makerere, Julia—I'm constantly reminded that I can never dream too big. Every time I met someone who had achieved more in life—whether education or career or business or family—my eyes were opened to how much further I could go. I looked beyond their success and examined how they got to where they were, what steps they took to climb higher. They showed me what I had never thought possible before and challenged me to push myself to climb to the same heights and beyond. Now every opportunity is a classroom where I learn more about myself and how I can push myself to go further. The moment I put a cap on what is possible, the impossible comes along and lets me know I can be a part of it. I am no one special. But the people who came around me saw what I could do if given the chance. Many times their dream for me was what got me through. Every one of us has the potential within ourselves to do more, to dream bigger, and to encourage others to dream big. I was about to discover how far those dreams would take me.

eleven

Without Borders

My family came up from Nyabikoni for my graduation from Makerere University. My siblings and my father rode on a bus, but I think my mother floated the whole way; she was so happy. Aunts and uncles on my mom's side also came to Kampala, which felt a little off to me since I wasn't that close with any of them. But they came and everyone cheered when I crossed the stage to receive my diploma. Afterward we celebrated, and they all told me how proud they were of me. The whole time my mom could not stop looking at me with a huge smile on her face and tears in her eyes. It was a great weekend for everyone, but something didn't sit well with me.

I never planned to celebrate my graduation, just as I did not celebrate graduating from high school, but my family pushed to mark the occasion with festivities. It seemed that my family wanted a moment to feel proud, but I couldn't escape the sense that I was being taken advantage of. After all that had happened, where I came from and where I was headed next, I wanted a quiet day of reflection by myself. All these feelings made for an awkward weekend. I could not help but look around at all the proud supporters and think to myself, *Where were you when I was struggling?*

It was hardest for me to have my father around that weekend. Even though I had given God my anger and bitterness toward my dad, I could not help but shake my head at the sight of him there, in Kampala, on my college campus, cheering for the son he had wished dead. He never told me he regretted what he said to me. He never asked for forgiveness. He never acknowledged the abuse that affected me every day. He acted like the pain he had inflicted on me never happened. Honestly, I did not expect anything more from him. He was, and he is, who he has always been. I had done the difficult, internal work on myself to be able to accept him for who he is, but that didn't make it any easier for me to see him cheering for me like a proud father. It was a hard time in my life, but I've come to realize that the past and his behavior are on him. He has to make peace with his own history; I couldn't do it for him graduation weekend, and I can't do that for him today.

On the other hand, watching my mom soak up my accomplishments did bring me joy. For everyone else, the day was about me, but for me, this day was about my mother. My achievement brought her honor, and in Africa, that's the most important thing. After this day, no one in Nyabikoni would ever look at her the same. Now she was an honored mother in the village, with a college graduate for a son and four other children following close behind.

Before my family returned to Nyabikoni, my mom gave me a huge hug. "I'm so proud of you, Peter," she said.

"Thanks, Mom." I loved being with her, and I was so grateful for her unwavering love, but the parading of my achievements had come to an end. I wanted to be out of the spotlight, get back to my life, and have my space. My reality was not their reality any longer.

"What are you going to do now?" she asked.

I thought for a moment and gave her a reassuring smile. "I'll keep working and see what opens up."

"Something will. Just you wait and see," she said.

Once my family left, I finally had time to sit and reflect. I could not help thinking, *What now?* Makerere University had always been about more than a degree for me. Here I found human acceptance and comradery unlike anything I had ever experienced. That had been my dream since my first days at Katweha School. Now I knew I could make it in life because I belonged with many other overachievers. But what did "making it in life" mean for me? A job? A family? *What's next?* I asked myself. Little did I know, the answer was about to unfold in a way I never imagined possible.

Mission to Mars

Just weeks after graduation, my pastor came to me with a request. "Peter, I have about a dozen students from Durham University in England coming here for a few weeks, but my schedule is packed and I am not available. Could you entertain them for me?" Our church did a lot of work with various international child advocacy groups, which made us a hub for short-term mission teams from Europe and the United States.

I laughed. "Entertain them?"

"You know what I mean. Take them to the different churches and neighborhoods around the city where they're going to work with kids. They're also going to help with some day camps and Vacation Bible School programs. You work with our kids and know what they need, so you'd be a big help with both of those. And if you could also show them around during their free time and maybe hang out with them at night when you aren't working, I'd really appreciate that. And, of course, I need you to be their interpreter. You spend as much time with Americans as you do with Ugandans. You speak English almost like it's your native tongue."

I wanted to help my pastor, but I didn't really have much extra time. I still worked nights as a radio operator for the International Committee of the Red Cross along with working part-time day shifts for another relief and child advocacy group. I had looked for a full-time job, but I discovered another hard reality of life in Uganda: it's not what you know but who you are related to that matters. All the really good jobs went to sons and daughters or nieces and nephews of those in charge. Because Uganda had an unemployment rate that hovered close to 80 percent, there weren't many good jobs to begin with, which meant that even though I had a fresh business degree from Makerere University, my opportunities were limited.

In spite of my time being tight and having some reservations about hosting yet another group of privileged missionaries who didn't fully understand the Ugandan way of life, I still told my pastor, "Sure. I can do that for you. It will be my pleasure." I could have added, *I don't sleep much anyway.*

The mission team arrived. Steven, the chaplain leader of the group, introduced himself. He was the only one who was not a student. "I graduated from Oak Hill College before going to work with students at Durham," he explained. He then had everyone in the group tell me a little about themselves, their names, majors, and why they had come on this trip. Every single one of them had that look in their eye and that confidence in their voice that announced, *I'm here to save the world!* No one came out and said these words, but I knew what they were thinking. All I could think was, *Oh boy, here we go again.* I saw that same look in every member of every mission team that came through our church, especially those from America. When you come from a church culture that equates affluence with God's blessing on your life, I guess it is only natural to assume that a very poor country must also be spiritually dark. For the group from Durham, that assumption lasted about twenty-four hours.

Our first day we loaded up on a bus and drove to a church located in the heart of one of Kampala's slums. The group planned to conduct a Bible day camp, and they were excited when we left the hotel. The group quieted down and seemed heartbroken by the time we reached the church. Looking out the bus windows at one poor neighborhood after another has a way of doing that. Over and over I heard, "How can people live here?" "The trash . . . it's everywhere," and "Those kids . . ." at the sight of street kids begging. These sights were not triggering for me. I saw them every day. I had lived them.

We pulled up to the church, and a crowd of laughing and smiling kids gathered around our van. These kids can't watch television or go to the movies, so when white people come into the neighborhood, they become the biggest show in town. Everyone turns out for it.

Interacting with these kids put the confidence back in the team. By the time we got inside and met the pastor, their batteries were recharged and they were ready to go. We didn't have much time to set up before the kids around the van started filling up the church. By the time we were ready to start, the place was overflowing. Steven came over to me, grinning. "This is going to be great," he said.

I smiled and nodded. "Yes, it is," I said. I had a feeling Steven and the rest had no idea what was about to take place.

The day camp kicked off with worship songs, and these kids sang! Their joy rocked the building. The mission team started teaching their lessons, and the kids didn't just respond; they actively participated. The more the team interacted with them, the more they saw how a lot of these kids knew the Bible by heart. Game time came—you always have to have game times when you work with kids—and the kids laughed and played; their joy was a powerful expression for anyone to behold.

By the time day camp ended and the team said their goodbyes to the children, I knew that a switch had been flipped. This team had come to transform the lives of these children, but it was the children who had rocked this mission team's world. Over the next three weeks, I took them to more neighborhoods and more slums where the team met more and more children and more and more adults who all deeply loved God. At night I had long conversations with different members of the team. They needed someone to help them process what they were seeing. "I thought I understood what faith was before I came, but I had no idea," I was told over and over. "These people who have so little have to trust God for everything. Their lives are so hard, and yet they still love God. I don't know that I have ever walked by faith like these people do every day. I came here to change their lives, but instead, they have changed mine." When I heard that, I knew my time had been well spent.

The team had a few days off. On one of their free days, Steven asked me to go with them on a safari. Everyone seemed really excited about going. I told them, sure, I'd love to go, but inside I kept thinking this had to be some sort of tourist fascination. Safaris were expensive. Why pay that kind of money when you can see all the giraffes and elephants and impalas you want for free along the highway from Kampala to Rwanda?

"Have you ever been on a safari before?" Steven, the leader of the group, asked.

"No. Never," I said. *Not officially, but unofficially at least fifty times going back to when I was ten,* I thought to myself.

"This will be a great opportunity for all of us then," Steven said.

"Sure," I said.

Everyone seemed to have a good time during the safari. Once or twice someone's eyes grew wide at the sight of a monkey. "Have you ever seen something like this so close up?" one girl asked.

I smiled. "A few times," I replied, not telling her that monkeys were an everyday sight in my home village.

Three weeks passed, and the student group prepared to go home. We exchanged email addresses and promised to stay in touch. The next day they got on a plane bound for

England, and I went back to my translation work during the day and coordinating transportation for the ICRC at night.

To my pleasant surprise, an email from Steven showed up in my inbox almost right away. "Hey, Peter. Just wanted to let you know how much we appreciated everything you did for us while we were there. We will talk more soon."

Over the course of the next few weeks, Steven and I exchanged emails on a regular basis. Some of the other team members emailed me as well.

Then, several months after the team had gone back to England, I saw an email from Steven in my inbox. I clicked on it. What I saw blew me away. "Would you be interested in coming to England and studying at Oak Hill College in London?" he asked.

I pushed back from my computer. My mind flashed back to the day James asked me if I was interested in going to school. Back then, James might as well have asked me if I wanted to go to the moon. And now I read, *Would you be interested in coming to England and studying in London?* If Katweha was the moon, going to England was Mars, that's how ridiculous and crazy and completely unexpected this offer was. A poor street kid going to school was crazy enough. For this street kid to graduate from high school and the university, that was crazier still. But now, for this same Ugandan street kid to go study at a prestigious college in England? I don't have words to explain how off the charts this sounded to me.

I laughed in disbelief, but since I had already gone to the moon, flying up to Mars was entirely possible. I gathered my thoughts and replied, "Absolutely, but I don't know how I could afford to go there."

Even though I worked two or three jobs, I still had to scrape by. I shared an apartment with a revolving door of roommates and sent money home for my siblings' education. Just saving up the money for the airplane ticket would take so long that I'd be ready to retire before I could actually go.

"We think we may have some ways around that," Steven replied. "All I need to know right now is whether or not you are interested?"

"Yes. Of course."

Steven sent me a packet from Oak Hill with a class catalogue, forms, and flyers along with instructions for how to apply for admission. I scrolled through all their programs and found a crisis management major. The words nearly jumped off the screen at me. Between war, disease, famine, and genocide, crisis was a way of life in central Africa. During my trips to Rwanda, I felt so helpless. I constantly wondered if I was making any difference at all. And now I found this, crisis management. *This is a degree that will open doors*, I thought. Not doors to moneymaking opportunities but doors to understanding people and how best to help them when their lives fall apart. I couldn't imagine a better course of study.

I applied and was accepted by Oak Hill. The admissions department helped guide me through the process of applying for the proper scholarships as well as my student visa. In the meantime, I continued working my part-time jobs and hanging out with friends when I could.

In the middle of this time, my supervisor from the ICRC approached me. "I'd like for you to accompany one of our teams into Sudan and visit a refugee camp. This will give you a better understanding of how everything operates."

"That sounds great," I said. Even though I'd visited many camps in Rwanda, almost all the camps were filled with children because the agency I went with focused primarily on child advocacy. The ICRC worked in some of the biggest refugee camps in the world, and nearly two decades of civil war had left Sudan with huge refugee populations both inside and outside the country. Unfortunately, war never seems to end there. Today, their latest civil war has displaced more than six million Sudanese.

A few days later, I climbed into one of a caravan of semis, all with "International Committee of the Red Cross" written along the sides of their trailers, and started north toward Sudan. I learned my lesson from my trips to Rwanda. I made sure I had my passport with me. Five or six hours later, we pulled into the first camp just across the Uganda-Sudan border. The size of the camp astounded me. Tents stretched out forever, and yet every inch of space between them was squeezed full of people. Adults milled around with nothing to do, their sadness, stress, and worry clear on their faces. The truck I was in started down one of the roads that went through the camp, but we had to stop quickly. The driver gave a small toot of his horn, and the group of kids who had been playing soccer in the road moved over to the side. As soon as we passed, I looked back in my mirror. The soccer game went on in the road like we had never been there. I saw the same scene on every road in the camp. African kids love soccer, and the dirt road through the camp provided the only empty space to play.

We finally reached the place where we needed to off-load our supplies. I jumped out and went around to the back of the trailer to help. Once everything was unloaded, I started walking to the ICRC office. On the way, I noticed another soccer game. One of the players did not quite fit in: a very white, shirtless kid who looked to be about eighteen. I went over and introduced myself to him. His name was Solomon, and he was from Southern California. "What are you doing all the way over here so far from home?" I asked.

"Missions. Trying to make a difference," he said. "I'm a student, but I'm taking some time off to get real-world experience." I asked when he planned to return to the US. "I don't know yet," he replied.

Solomon and I ended up spending a lot of time together, not just that day but throughout my time in the camp. He worked with kids, and like everywhere else, the kids were drawn to me. Before I left, I told Solomon, "If you get homesick, you should come down and visit me in Kampala. My roommate is American and so is my girlfriend, if you want to hang out. We can also treat you to some American food."

Solomon told me he loved the sound of that. We exchanged phone numbers. A couple of weeks later, he called and ended up staying with me and my roommate, Will, for four weeks. Then Solomon went back to the refugee camps and soon I headed off to England, but we stayed in touch.

These Are the Voyages

All the details for studying at Oak Hill came together. The college granted me a scholarship, which covered almost all of my expenses, and the Durham team that had come to Uganda helped with my plane ticket. My flight was an adventure. I had never seen an airplane up close, much less boarded one. My only experience with airplanes came from watching them pass overhead in the sky. Today, I've flown hundreds of thousands of miles all over the world, but on my first trip, I couldn't believe how many people were waiting to get on the plane at the airport terminal. The surprises kept coming when I stepped into the plane. I had no idea you could actually walk around or watch movies.

But the airplane wasn't as big of a shock to my system as the English roads. Steven and a couple of other guys I knew picked me up at the airport when I first arrived in London. I put my bags in the trunk of Steven's car (or should I say the "boot," since I was in England?), and we took off toward the school. Everyone tried to carry on a conversation with me, and I talked as much as I could, but the car kept going faster and faster. The faster we went, the less I talked. I glanced out the window. All the cars were going very fast. *How does anyone survive?* I wondered. It wasn't the speed that bothered me. I was much more worried about what was going to happen when our car traveling seventy miles per hour dropped down into one of the crater-sized potholes that cover nearly every road in and around Kampala. "What's wrong, Peter?" someone finally asked.

"How can you go this fast and avoid the potholes?" I asked.

Steven laughed. "Our roads are a little better over here."

As a student, I was allowed to work twenty hours per week in the United Kingdom. I found a job with a moving company on the weekends, and at night I worked for a food prep company. I got really good at chopping onions for London restaurants. Of course, I also went to class and studied and did my best to take advantage of the opportunity I had been given.

Solomon and I kept in touch through email and occasional phone calls. Fifteen months after I had moved to England, he went back to school in California. He called me during that time and said, "I know you have a degree in business already, and you're working on a degree in crisis management, but do you have any interest in coming to California to study? My college has a program that focuses on how you can change the lives of others on a more personal level. What do you say? You want to come study here after you've finished up in England?"

"Come on, Solomon. You have to be kidding. I can't just move to the United States. It's expensive, and visas are very hard to get for someone from Africa. And why ask me to come there? What made you even think about doing something like this for me?" I felt like Solomon's invitation came more out of a sense of adventure and our friendship than from any specific program at the college he attended.

"I saw your heart while we were together in the camps. I know you love kids, and you want to help others any way you can. I really think you should come. What do you think?"

If moving to England was a trip to Mars, this was now a ticket on the starship *Enterprise* with Captain Kirk and Mister Spock. Did I want to study in California? "Yeah. Sure. I'd love that, but how much does it cost?"

"I've already talked to my school about you. They'll find a way to make this happen."

"Okay," I said, "I'm in." My shock started turning into excitement. "Yeah, let's do this. It sounds great." I still had a little more than a semester to finish at Oak Hill, but California seemed like it could be a real possibility.

Solomon sent everything I needed to apply for school. Once again, I applied to a school in a country I could hardly imagine and was happy to find out the college accepted me. The school also awarded me a scholarship, which meant I did not have to worry about how to pay for tuition. However, I still had to get a visa. I could not do that from England. I had to return to Kampala and apply in person at the American Embassy. I made a few phone calls first. Thanks to Julia's introductions while I was at Makerere, I knew many of the officials at the embassy, including those who worked with Ugandans trying to go to the US. These weren't just my friends. I had worked with their children in our church. I called one of them. "Sure, I can help you with that, Peter," he said, "but I am about to be transferred to Israel. I don't know who will take my place."

My heart sank. The visa process for the United States is very complicated and can be difficult to navigate. On top of that, those in charge can feel barraged by the number of people hoping to quickly finalize a student visa. My friend at the embassy couldn't just hand me a visa, but because he knew me so well, he was willing to help me through the process, whereas a stranger might have just pointed to a stack of forms and told me to fill them out.

"What can we do?" I asked.

"Listen, you helped my kids so much that I want to return the favor. Start filling out forms and get them here as quickly as you can. Maybe we can get this wrapped up before my transfer," he said.

I flew back to Uganda for my visa interviews, received approval for a student visa, then flew back to England to finish my studies at Oak Hill. As soon as I graduated, I went home to Kampala and moved back in with one of my old room-mates for four months, then boarded a plane bound for Los Angeles. I planned to attend school, take more steps toward understanding my faith journey, and see what America was all about. I had no idea what awaited me, but I trusted it would all work out and opportunities would present themselves if I just walked through the open doors ahead of me. From Steven to Solomon, each person in my chain of hope extended friendship, offered life-changing invitations, and opened doors that took me places I never imagined visiting, much less living. Opportunities consistently came my way without my planning, and I tried to lean into this way of life, trusting even in the midst of ambiguity and grabbing hold of every chance I had to improve myself and learn. Little did I know the biggest surprise was yet to come.

twelve

Paying It Forward

About eight months after I moved to Murrieta, California, to attend college at Solomon's invitation, Derek, a friend I made at the school, came to me with an odd request. "I'm going to go check out another school, but I don't want to drive up there and stay by myself. Do you want to come with me?"

"Where is it?"

"Up in Santa Clarita."

"How far is that from here?" I asked.

"Depending on the time of day, it will take us three or four hours to drive there. It's up north in the Santa Clarita Valley above Los Angeles. We'll need to spend the night."

I didn't know which valley Derek was talking about, but I didn't think I had ever been there. Murrieta is inland, part of Riverside County, where it's always hot and dry. "Sure," I said. "I'm always up for seeing more of California." I had no idea how long I'd get to stay in the States, so I wanted to see as much of it as I could. When I attended Oak Hill College in England, I worked for a summer camp that allowed me to see Paris and other parts of Europe. I took full advantage of the transportation system and the ease to see so many notable sights.

The next day Derek picked me up early, and we headed north on Interstate 15. I quickly learned one of the key lessons of Southern California: the highways are great, but traffic barely moves. You can't get anywhere fast, even without potholes. On the way, I asked Derek to tell me about this school.

"It's called The Master's University."

The name meant nothing to me. Derek also mentioned the name of the university president, thinking I should recognize it. I didn't. I really didn't know much about any well-known people in any field outside of the celebrity actors I saw in the movies. When Julia and I dated, we'd go to movie nights at the American Embassy in Kampala.

"So, why do you want to go there?" I asked.

"They have a program I want to explore that they don't have at our school. And I've heard the campus is incredible."

After crawling along then speeding up then crawling along again for over one hundred miles, we finally arrived at The Master's University. Derek had heard right. The campus was beautiful. Green hills surrounded the campus, with mountains rising up beyond them. Everywhere I looked I saw lush trees and grass. The buildings all looked so new. "I've never seen a university like this," I said.

"I know," Derek replied. "Now you can see why I want to come here."

We found a place to park and went into one of the buildings. The two of us wandered from building to building until somehow we ended up in the admissions office. Derek had run into a professor in the hallway, but I kept moving into the entryway. A woman behind the main desk said hello. "I'm Lisa, an admissions counselor here."

"Hello," I replied. "Nice to meet you."

"How have you enjoyed your visit so far?" Lisa asked.

"We just got here, but I like what I've seen. This school seems really cool."

She smiled. "You know you can come here if you like."

"I already have a bachelor's degree in business and another in crisis management," I said.

"A lot of our students have degrees in other fields," she answered, "but they come here to expand their education from more of a faith perspective."

"That sounds interesting," I replied. I was really just making conversation while I waited for Derek to return.

"Would you like to go ahead and look over an application? You could fill it out while you're here," she said.

"I don't know. I am really just here with a friend. He's the one who's really interested in this school," I replied. "By the way, how much does it cost to attend here?"

"Each school year is approximately $24,000," Lisa said without blinking.

"Does that come with a house and a car too?" I asked almost like a reflex.

Lisa laughed. "No, that's just tuition."

"Okay," I said with a tone that made it clear this conversation was over.

She must've noticed my uncomfortable disposition. "We work very hard to make sure money doesn't get in the way of people following their dreams. We have several scholarships available, including scholarships for international students."

I hadn't told her I was from Uganda, but I was pretty sure my accent gave me away.

Lisa flipped through some papers. "Hmmm, let's see. Today is Tuesday. It looks like the deadline for international students to apply for scholarships is this Friday. That gives you plenty of time if you want to go ahead and apply."

Derek ended up talking to a few other students and friends, and I had nothing to do but sit. I decided I might as well fill out the paperwork. "Sure," I said to Lisa. "I'll fill out an application."

I went outside and sat under a nearby oak tree. I could hardly believe I was applying to another university in America. While I liked the small school I was at in Murrieta, it wasn't accredited like The Master's University; that was a big plus. Derek and I left the beautiful campus wondering if we might be headed to Santa Clarita for the next school year.

A week later, a really friendly person from the registrar's office called me. I had been accepted. "That's great," I said, "but I cannot afford to come. Nothing has changed with my finances in the past week."

"Well, that's the best news," she said. "You have been awarded a $17,000 scholarship."

The woman sounded very excited about this news, but $17,000 still left $7,000 for me to come up with, and my student visa allowed me to work only a very limited number of hours. What little money I made I lived on and sent back to my family in Uganda. Seven thousand dollars might as well have been $7 million.

"I appreciate the offer," I said, "but I don't have $7,000 to make up the rest of the bill, and I don't have any way to come up with that kind of money."

There was silence for a moment. I thought we would say our goodbyes, but then I heard, "Let's not give up so easily, Peter. What church do you attend in California?" I told her the name. "We have a matching scholarship program in place. That means The Master's University will match whatever your church might be willing to give toward your education. Let me give them a call, and we'll see what we can come up with."

Even though I had been a part of the California church for only a few months, they gave half of what I needed and the university matched the other half. I had never planned on going to The Master's University, but then again, I never planned on going to Katweha School or Makerere or Oak Hill or any of the other places life had taken me. People today ask me how I got to where I am now. I look back on this crazy journey, and after all the years of reflection and wrestling, I have only one answer: God. He put the right people in my life at the right time. I owe everything I have to Providence and the kindness of strangers. Yes, I have worked very hard. I pushed myself at Katweha, which opened the door for me to go to Makerere University. I also worked very hard there to earn my degree, just as I did at Oak Hill. But without the kindness of strangers who first opened the door for me to go in and achieve, I'd still be on the streets of Kampala with no hope, no dreams, no life.

New Career Path

At the beginning of every school year, The Master's University Board of Governors invites one student to speak at a dinner they hold. My first year that keynote speaker turned out to be me. Apparently, the board consisted of many important people, especially notable figures in sports and entertainment. Their celebrity status was lost on me. I had no idea who anyone was. I was seated near the university president, who introduced himself, then asked, "Do you like baseball, Peter?"

I thought it was an odd question. "That's not really a sport we play in Uganda," I replied.

"Well, we'll have to get you to a game sometime," he replied. Then he nodded to the man sitting next to me. "That guy, he can take you."

I didn't understand what was going on. The man next to me stuck out his hand. "Hey, Peter. Nice to meet you. I'm Kevin." It turned out that Kevin was Kevin Malone, the general manager of the Los Angeles Dodgers. I still don't know much about baseball, but Kevin and I became fast friends after that first meeting. He and his family became my adopted family in California.

After dinner, the program began. A few speakers took turns. Then the president introduced me. My stomach did a couple of flips. I had never given a formal talk to a group of adults before. My little public speaking experience came from teaching children, and these weren't children.

I stood up to speak; calmness washed over me from head to toe. I felt like I had done this my entire life. I thanked the group for inviting me to speak to them. "I am incredibly grateful for the opportunity you have given this kid from Africa to come and study at such an incredible school. I have studied at colleges in Uganda and England, and The Master's University is simply amazing.

"Coming here, I have learned more about my God. This school has such a solid theology department, but you know, I come from a world where many, many people cannot read, and those that can read are lucky if they have a Bible. I come from a place filled with extreme poverty and hardships and disease. My country has been torn apart by war and the lasting legacy of a dictator who abused his power; hundreds of thousands of people simply disappeared because they disagreed with him. In Uganda, people struggle to understand the most basic truth of the Bible, and that is God loves them in the midst of their day-to-day struggle just to survive.

"I also made over fifty trips into Rwanda immediately after the genocide where eight hundred thousand people were killed in one hundred days. Many of those who did the killing still live alongside the surviving family members of those who died. In Rwanda, people are not arguing over denominational differences or Calvinism and Arminianism. They don't care about different theories regarding the second coming of Jesus. They are trying to reconcile and forgive one another and move forward as a nation. They wrestle with the reality of a loving God in the midst of such heartache.

"I come from a world of poverty and death, a world filled with people who God loves just as much as he loves Americans. Sometimes it is hard to grasp the vastness of God's love. And it is also hard for us here, in this American academic setting, to remember that simple principles about God's nature and his desire for humanity to live in peace are the questions the rest of the world wants answers for. I hope we never lose sight of that. I came here to understand God's mercy and his grace, his love and his forgiveness. That's what I hope to take back to my country after my time here, and I hope that's what you will inspire your students to strive for."

I had poured out my heart and expressed for the first time the questions that I had carried around inside my head most of my life. *Is God real? If he is, why is there such suffering in the world? Why is there so much hatred?* People in America may struggle with the same questions, but they take on greater weight when you live in a world filled with poverty, hunger, war, and genocide. That is what I wanted the people in this room to understand. I had a chance to put a spotlight on how people in Africa were struggling with the realness of God and trying to live out his grace and forgiveness in difficult situations. I could not ignore this opportunity to challenge these men and women in the same way God had challenged me.

The next day all of the students at the university assembled for a special gathering where the university president planned to speak. I was not prepared for what he was about to say. Rather than launching into a speech, he began, "Yesterday I met a special student. Peter, where are you?"

Oh no! I thought. I sort of raised my hand in a way that I hoped wouldn't be seen. I wanted to vanish away, but he saw me.

"Peter, will you come up here and take a couple of minutes to explain to the rest of the student body why you are excited to be here and maybe what you are concerned about in your home country?"

I had given the first speech of my life less than twenty-four hours earlier, but I had weeks to prepare for it. Now I had to stand up and say something without time to even think about what I should say. I slowly walked up on the stage, hoping not to embarrass myself.

The university president handed me a microphone, then stepped back to let me speak. I took a deep breath, then shared, "I appreciate the opportunity to speak to all of you. You know, every single one of us is blessed to be here. Most of you have parents who love you and have done everything they can for you to enjoy the best education you can get and for you to pursue your dreams. But where I come from, we don't have that. Going to school, much less going on to college, is a dream that the vast majority of kids will never have because their parents are too poor to send them even though the cost is very low compared to America. Little girls have even less of a chance for education. They are viewed as third-class citizens. Boys can work in the fields, but for girls, their parents wait for them to turn fourteen so that they can marry them off and remove the burden of feeding them. Even if they want to go to school, they cannot. That door is forever closed.

"I hope you grasp the privilege and the responsibility and the gift you have been given. I hope you enjoy this opportunity and do not waste what your parents have given you. I hope you understand the greatest need people in the world have today is to understand God's mercy and his grace and that you take seriously his command to love one another.

"I come from a very poor country and a very poor family where we struggled to survive. But at the same time, we still love God and hope in his goodness. I hope that in the midst of the affluence that surrounds us here, you will continue to love God and have a passion for him."

A week later, a student named Rick approached me. "I was really touched by what you shared last week."

"Thank you," I replied.

"Yeah, it really got me thinking about how more people need to hear this and take action. My dad is a pastor up in Arrowhead. We have a special event every year when child advocacy speakers come and talk to our community about helping vulnerable children. We give everyone the opportunity to sponsor a child in need. My dad wants you to come and speak." Sponsoring a child means someone in the West gives money every month for a specific child in the developing world to help that child reach their potential. The money helps provide for their basic needs: education, health, nutrition, and social skills.

I didn't have to think about it. "Of course, I will speak. But you know, I don't drive."

"That's not a problem," Rick said. "I'll drive you there and back."

Sunday came. Rick picked me up and drove me to his father's church. Nearly five hundred people gathered in the mountains of Arrowhead, California. When my time came, I talked about what it was like to grow up in extreme poverty in Uganda. I did not hold back. "Here in America one of our biggest problems is overeating. In the village where I grew up, that was never a problem. Families are blessed if they have one meal a day. Many only have enough food for a meal every other day. That's just the reality of life in rural Uganda."

I spoke for nearly twenty minutes. Afterward people in the church came to me and thanked me for what I had said. I could tell by their faces that they wanted to say more. Finally, one woman had the courage to ask, "When you talked about families that could afford only one meal every other day, was that, uh, how do I ask this . . . ?"

"It's okay," I said. "Yes, I lived in one of those families that ate only every other day. We felt blessed to have that." It was the first time I had shared any of my own experiences with anyone. I did not tell my friends at Katweha School what it was like in my village. No one at Makerere University knew I had lived on the streets for almost six years. My friends in England probably assumed I grew up in one of the wealthier families in Uganda. How else could I have graduated high school and gone on to college? I never told them any different.

But now, looking at the tears welling up in this woman's eyes, I felt safe to say more. She could see my story had a happy ending. I think her tears were for the millions of children who are not as lucky as I was.

"What did you . . . I mean, on the other days . . . did you . . ."

"On the other days we went hungry," I said as gently as I could.

The woman hugged me, then walked over to the table with the sponsorship cards lying on it and selected a card with a child's photo on it. "God bless you, Peter," she said on her way out.

Before Rick and I drove back down the mountain to Santa Clarita, his dad came over, a huge grin on his face. "Peter, thank you. We have these events every year, but this year our church committed to sponsoring two hundred children."

"That's great," I said. Then I thought for a moment. "So, how many kids normally get sponsored on one of these Sundays?"

179

Rick's dad smiled. "Not even close to two hundred. We're going to have you back next year, if you'll come."

"Yes, of course," I said.

When I got back to my dorm, I started thinking about those two hundred children. *Two hundred!* I had not done anything particularly special. All I did was talk about what I had experienced. My twenty minutes in front of the church put a living, breathing face on the sponsorship cards people filled out.

Sitting in my room, alone, reflecting on what had just happened, my past came back to me, but not as something bad and traumatic I needed to put behind me. If I had not gone through everything I experienced, growing up in a poor family, the beatings from my father, running away and living on the streets of Kampala, then being found and rescued by James, I would not be here right now. Every heartache, every struggle, every trauma I suffered changed my heart and opened my eyes to those who suffer just as I did. *If I had not lived through the nightmare I escaped when James took me to Katweha, what would have become of the two hundred children who were sponsored today?* I thought. *And how many more can my story help?*

For the first time, I became grateful for all I had been through. Not eating every day. Working with my mother in the garden. Watching my siblings. Hustling for food in Kampala. Finding ways to sleep on the street. Each of these experiences were hard, but they also shaped me into who I am and developed a heart of compassion within me. Children all over the world live through hell on earth. They suffer in poverty. They die of disease and neglect. Millions of children live through what I lived through and even worse. The only difference between them and me is that I had survived and was now in a position to tell their stories by telling mine. These vulnerable children could now be seen and heard and known through me. And if that could result in hundreds more, or thousands more, being sponsored and helped so they could begin to dream, then everything I had ever been through was worth it. I would not change one thing. In this moment, I realized the power of my story and the unique opportunity I had to bring life-changes to so many children if I had the confidence to speak up and use my past for good.

A few days after speaking in Arrowhead, Rick's dad called. "Is it okay for me to give your phone number to one of the child advocacy organizations we partnered with on Sunday?"

I was a little puzzled by his question. "Sure, but why do they want to talk to me?"

"They called me after receiving all the commitment cards from Sunday's service. They've never had a response like this in any of the churches they've worked with. He wanted to know what we did. I told him we had a student from Uganda who goes to The Master's University come out and speak. I think they want you to do more speaking for them."

My weekends suddenly became very busy. The nonprofit organization paid my expenses to go all over the country speaking to groups. Each time I spoke, more people came to me and asked about my life. The conversations became more and more comfortable for me. I knew these were caring and compassionate people. They did not look down on me or feel sorry for me because of what I had lived through. Their concern was genuine. And every time I answered their questions and told them more about my personal experiences, they picked up cards and sponsored kids. Every time.

Not all the questions I was asked were sensitive to my Ugandan reality. I had a teenage boy come up after one of my talks and ask, "So, what kind of shoes did you have over there? What were your favorite ones?"

"I didn't have a favorite pair of shoes," I said. "I did not receive my first pair of shoes until I was sixteen."

The kid sort of shook his head. "Why?"

"Because no one in my village could afford to buy shoes."

The kid walked away with a look on his face that told me I had just blown his mind.

Another time someone asked me if I had a favorite food growing up. I wondered if they had listened to my talk at all. "No," I replied.

"Why?"

"Well, I grew up in a place where there was no food. My favorite food was whatever I could find to eat."

Dream Job

I continued speaking at events around the United States the entire time I went to The Master's University. After my graduation, another international child advocacy organization approached me about coming to work for them full-time. When I told the team for whom I had served as a speaker that I planned to take the other job, they said, "Hold on. Don't accept anything yet."

Within a matter of hours, they called me back and offered me a job. "We don't know exactly what the job is going to look like, but all we know is we want you working with us." A few days later, I met with their leadership team, and we came up with an entirely new job description based on my experiences and my gifts. They wanted me to continue to speak, but they had something even bigger in mind. "We'd like for you to take key groups of donors and influencers around the world to see and experience our work in the field."

When I lived with James and his family, I had met groups like this as they came through to visit Uganda. I had even helped James show some people around. I knew the impact a trip like this could make. "This sounds exactly like the job I am looking for. When do I start?" A few years earlier when I escorted the group of students from England around Uganda, I saw how these trips transformed those who took them. I never dreamed they'd have the same impact on me.

Once I settled into my job, I spent more time on an airplane than I did in my own apartment. I took groups to South America, Africa, and Asia. I spent time in camps in Haiti, Peru, and Columbia. We toured villages in India, Kenya, and Zimbabwe. Over the course of a decade, I made somewhere between two hundred and three hundred trips to different parts of the world, and everywhere I went I saw one constant: my childhood experience was not unique. I saw villages that made Nyabikoni look wealthy. I met children on the streets amid the destruction caused by earthquakes and hurricanes in Port-au-Prince, Haiti, who were far worse off than I had ever been. Those trips changed the way I looked at my past. I thought my life was bad, but compared to the worst of the worst, I was blessed.

My perception of those who live in affluent nations also changed. My job was basically to make worlds collide. I took those who had so much into a world of those who had nothing. Over and over I stood back amazed at the results. I took famous and successful people from the worlds of entertainment, sports, business, and religion into areas with severe poverty beyond what they could imagine. Rather than shrink back from it, these people had their hearts moved. And they gave. They didn't just give money and get back to their normal lives. I saw people commit to making a permanent difference. I also saw lives change in those villages as a result. And that's what made this my dream job. By connecting the haves with the have-nots, I had the privilege of seeing real transformation take place in the lives of both. I could not think of a better way to invest my time here on earth.

And that's where my story could have easily ended. I now had the life I first dreamed about while playing cards with my friends in our dorm at Katweha School. I was paying it forward, doing for others what James had done for me but on a worldwide scale. James, my teachers, Julia, and Solomon didn't know what their invitations would lead to in my life. Their actions, though seemingly small and "normal," had massive effects, not only on me but on thousands of children throughout the world. I never imagined there was one more surprise waiting for me, one that turned my entire life upside down.

thirteen

What Does It Mean to Give It All?

"Our bus is here. It's time to get going," I announced to the group of senior pastors from Texas waiting in the Nairobi hotel lobby with me. Nine years had passed since I had accepted my dream job and stepped into the American dream, but I still enjoyed taking influencers on these trips. Every trip and every speech I gave reaffirmed why I took this job in the first place. Since I spoke for the first time at the church in Arrowhead, more than ten thousand children had been sponsored through my work. I didn't just talk to others about sponsoring children. I sponsored many myself. If I didn't practice what I preached, I might as well have kept my mouth shut.

My group filed out of the hotel lobby and onto our bus. Once everyone was seated, I announced, "Hey, everyone, this is Mark, our driver. Mark, this is everyone." My group said hello, and Mark smiled and waved. A couple of pastors said something like "How ya doin'?" in their thick Texas accents. Mark just smiled. He understood a little English, but I'm not sure what he thought of that Texas drawl.

"So, our drive is going to be about two hours until we reach Kijabe. The roads are a little bumpy over here, so I don't recommend leaning up against the window to take a nap," I said with a little laugh. My group laughed along with me. I wasn't sure how many of them, if any, had made a trip like this before. The first day was always the hardest on first-timers, not the travel but the extreme poverty they were about to witness. Once you spend any time at all in a rural African village, you're never the same.

"Okay, Mark, I think we are ready. Let's go," I said before dropping down into a seat next to a young guy named Jason Johnson. Little did I know that my randomly choosing to sit next to him was going to be as life-changing as spotting James in the Kampala market a lifetime ago.

What? Why?

"What do you think of Kenya so far?" I asked Jason.

"The hotel was nice, and breakfast was pretty good. Haven't seen much else than that so far," he said with a laugh.

"You will today," I replied.

"That's why we're here, right?" Jason said. He paused for a moment. "You know, I almost canceled on you at the last minute. Hated to do that though, so here I am."

Now he had my curiosity up. "What's going on?"

"My wife and I have a little one at home who just joined our family. I could hardly pull myself away from her. Do you want to see her picture?"

"Sure," I said, expecting to see a photo of a baby who looked a lot like Jason. My mind had trouble computing what I saw when he pulled out his phone. The child was a baby, maybe a few weeks old, but she didn't look like Jason. "Wait a minute. This is your child?"

"Yes."

"But she's black and you're . . ."

"White, I know," Jason said with a laugh. "My wife and I are foster parents. Brittany was placed with us right before I left. We plan to adopt her."

I had now lived in the United States for nearly fifteen years, and Jason was the first foster dad I had ever met. I'd heard the term before, but I never knew exactly what it meant. "So, what do you mean she was placed with you?" I asked.

"Child Protective Services removed her from her biological parents and brought her to our home. I don't know exactly why. Most kids end up in the foster care system because of neglect or their parents are on drugs, or both. Usually both. Sometimes they are simply abandoned, but that's most often because of drugs as well," Jason explained.

"Does this happen a lot?"

"Oh, yeah." Jason nodded. "Since the opioid crisis hit, it's become very common. The problem is there aren't enough foster families to take in all the kids. Some kids end up sleeping at the Department of Child Services office until they find a family. Some have been placed in juvenile detention facilities because states have no other place for them to go and be safe." He let out a sigh. "There are more churches in America than there are kids in foster care, so the math seems pretty simple on how to solve the problem. Unfortunately, fixing this isn't that easy. That's why my wife and I became foster parents. We had to do something. How could I ask my church members to sponsor vulnerable children in Africa and then ignore those who are right in our own backyard?"

I spent a lot of time with people from all walks of life on trips like this, going back to when I still lived in Uganda. In my experience—and to any pastors reading this book, please do not take this the wrong way—I have found a lot of pastors are very good at telling other people what to do, but they fall short when it comes to doing those same things themselves. Yet here was a man with a heart for vulnerable and abandoned children who not only talked about doing something but also went beyond sponsoring a child. This child who had no blood connection to him was now his daughter, and not just in name only. He was crazy about this once-abandoned baby girl with the deepest love any father ever had for his child.

I spent a lot of time talking with Jason over the next ten days. These trips were designed to create a passion for hurting and vulnerable children within the hearts of guests, but it was my heart that was moved. I could not get my head around the idea that in America, the richest country in the world, the land that people all over the continent of Africa look at as a heaven on earth, there were families who could not care for their own babies. I had made hundreds of trips around the world on behalf of children and families. But had I ever looked around where I lived? How could I have been so blind not to know that there were children in need of homes all around me? The more I thought about it, the more one question haunted me: *What are you going to do now?*

The Meaning of Sacrifice

I flew home to Denver, climbed into my Infiniti FX, and took off from the airport toward my apartment. Since 2003, I had really liked driving, and now I really liked my car. But I could not stop thinking, *If I have a child come into my home, I'll have to sell this car. Can I bring myself to do that? Haven't I worked hard for it? Why should I give it up?*

My apartment wasn't in the fanciest part of Denver, but it was a nice area. I walked in and looked around. I had two bedrooms, one for sleep and the other for my office. *There's no way I can bring a child here. I'd need more room. And besides, this place isn't set up for children. I'd probably need a house. I can't afford a house in the Denver area. Can I leave my home for the sake of caring for a child?*

I lived very simply. I made a deliberate decision not to clutter my life with a lot of stuff. All of my clothes could fit into two bags. Beyond my clothes, I owned a set of skis for Colorado winters and a bike for the summer. And my car. That was it. That was all I needed, and I was happy. But if I became a foster dad, I couldn't get by with so little. *Do I really want to make such a radical change to my life?*

I argued with myself. It wasn't like I wasn't already making a huge difference in the lives of children. One of my first trips in my dream job had taken me back to Uganda. I led a group to a village so remote that the children there had never seen a white person before. The sight of a dozen white faces scared the kids, especially one little boy who was about five years old. When he saw my group, he hid behind me. I didn't know he was there until he reached up and took hold of my pinky finger; he didn't let go. He melted my heart. He was dirty and naked and clearly not well. I asked one of our workers in the village about him. "Yeah, he's a really sad story," the worker said. "He's HIV positive. Who knows how long he has left." Like me at his age, he had no future.

"Is he sponsored by someone?" I asked.

"No. He has a couple of older siblings, and one of them is sponsored. You know the rules. Only one child per family." Most international relief agencies allow sponsorship for only one child in each family so that a greater number of families can be helped. The thinking is that by helping one child in the family, usually the youngest, the entire family will reap some benefit.

"But if he has HIV, that means at least his mother and probably both of his parents are infected too, right?" I said.

"Most likely, yes," the worker said.

The whole time we talked, the little boy kept a tight grip on my finger. I finally told the worker, "I think we can figure out a way to help this little guy."

Our team made sure he had what he needed to get by, and it worked. He did not die of AIDS. The United States started a program that made antiviral drugs available all over Africa, and that, along with regular nutrition that came from him being sponsored, saved his life.

I had been devoting my entire career to changing the lives of hurting and vulnerable children, kids who were just like me when I was a boy. I thought helping financially was a giant leap toward creating a brighter future. Hadn't I done enough?

But then Brittany's photo flashed in my mind. I could see Jason proudly showing her off, a proud father who could not wait to get home to his little girl. *Where would Brittany be without Jason and his wife?* I wondered. *And how many more Brittanys are out there?* I knew I was making a difference in the lives of children, but everything I did kept those children at a safe distance. I made my trips and sent my checks, and at the end of the day, I came home and closed my mind. I did not have to think about any of them until the next check was due or until the next trip started. *Is my life really devoted to making a difference in the lives of those who are most vulnerable when what I do requires zero sacrifice on my part?* I knew the answer. Now the question was, What was I going to do about it?

House Flipping Foster Dad

The first thing I did was leave my job. I could not be gone thirty weeks or more out of every year and raise a child. *Am I really doing this? Can I even do this? Can a single man be a foster dad?* I guess I was going to find out. Then I traded in my Infiniti for a van. I went from cool to soccer mom overnight. It's a good thing I wasn't trying to impress any single women with my wheels.

After trading in my car, I started looking to buy a house. Leaving your job and buying a house don't exactly go together, but that's what I knew I needed to do. I knew a lot of people around the country from my work, so I began to ask around. "Where's a good, cheap place to live where houses are affordable?" Denver definitely was not that place for me. Eventually, a friend connected me with one of his friends, a man named William, who turned out to be another in the long line of strangers whose kindness impacted my life. William invited me to come down and check out the Oklahoma City area. I explained why I had decided to make this move, to which William replied, "I work in real estate. You can come and work for us while you figure out your next steps."

As it turned out, William didn't just work in real estate. His company owned rentals all over the area. When people moved out of a house, or when the company acquired a new property, work always needed to be done on the house. When I started with William, I told him I wasn't looking for a fancy job. "I want to learn all the ins and outs of this business right there in the trenches so that I can start my own business doing this." Going back to when I used to sell nuts on the streets of my home village, I've had an entrepreneurial streak. I also had a business degree from Makerere University. I majored in business to make it possible to start my own business so that I could help others. But so many other opportunities had come my way that I never needed to put that plan into action—until now. I didn't want to learn the real estate business so that I could work for someone else. I knew there was money to be made in flipping houses. I could work for myself, set my own hours, and have plenty of time to be a dad.

All I knew about house flipping came from watching television. William changed that. I asked him to put me in the trenches, and that's exactly where I found myself. He put me to work on some of the worst of the worst properties. I worked with contractors. I figured out what materials we needed to make houses livable again. I hammered nails and replaced drywall and painted walls and everything else that went into making a house livable. I learned every part of the business that I could. After working for William for eight months, I took a big step that put all I had learned to the test: I bought my own house and started the renovation process. Now it was time to start stage 2 of my plan.

If you ask me, becoming a foster or adoptive dad is a lot harder than becoming a biological father. Jason had explained to me how you have to undergo multiple background checks, go through an interview process, take special classes, and have a social worker do home inspections in which they tell you what you have to change to make your house safe for a child. I think if people had to go through the same process to have biological children, the population might drop. I started the process after I bought my house. That way, by the time I reached the home inspection phase, my house would be completely renovated and ready to welcome a child.

Even after all I had done, I could not stop wondering, *Will the state of Oklahoma even let me become a foster dad?* I didn't think they would, at least not until I proved myself. I thought I could perhaps start out as a mentor to children and maybe graduate up to foster dad. I really had no idea how the system worked.

I made an appointment with Angels Foster Family Network and took along a friend to be my character reference. A social worker invited me in and introduced herself. "I'm Rachel. It's so nice to meet you. Now, how can I help you today?"

I wasn't quite sure what to say, so I blurted out, "I know the foster care system is overloaded with kids, and I wanted to find out if there's anything I could do to help, like maybe become a mentor to at-risk kids."

"Have you ever thought about becoming a foster parent?" Rachel asked.

"Yes, but I don't qualify," I said.

Rachel smiled. "Why?"

"Well, I'm a single man from Africa who has never been married and never had children."

"That doesn't matter. You can be a foster parent," Rachel said.

"All right. Wow!" I said. "Where do I sign up?"

I'm not sure Rachel ever had someone so eager to enlist. She pulled an application form out of her desk. "You start with this," she said as she handed it to me with a pen.

I filled out the form right there in her office. As soon as I finished it, I asked, "Okay. Now what?"

"Now I will connect you with one of our best social workers who will walk through the entire process with you."

Rachel took me downstairs and introduced me to the tallest woman I'd ever seen. I am only five feet seven inches tall. Esther the social worker looked to be close to seven feet tall. I craned my neck to look her in the eye and introduced myself. "Have a seat, Peter. Let's get started."

Over the next few months, Esther became my guide. She helped me sign up for the MAPP class, which stands for Model Approach to Partnership in Parenting. The class is designed to help prospective foster parents understand children who come out of trauma. Before the first class, I thought, *If they want to know about coming out of trauma, I can teach them a few things.* As it turns out, I had a *lot* more to learn than I ever imagined.

I walked in for my first class, and every head turned and every eye stared straight at me. For starters, I was the only single person in the room. I know everyone else had to be thinking I was nuts for even considering taking on the challenge of foster parenting by myself. Everyone also stared at me because I was the only black person in the room, the only person of any kind of color. *Okay, this is going to be interesting. The only single, black guy in a room full of middle-class, white married couples. We'll see how this goes.*

By the second class, I had forgotten all about being different. These classes did more than help me understand my future children. They opened my eyes to my own past. I had lived through trauma, but that didn't mean I understood it or how it had shaped me. I knew I had a hard time trusting people and that I had buttons that were easily pushed. The MAPP class helped me understand why. Every session took me on a journey that allowed me to understand myself and heal from my past while confronting things about myself that I had always tried to ignore. *Even if I never foster a single child, I needed this class,* I thought on my drive home each night. *I wish I could have taken this years ago.*

One class, however, nearly made me walk away. The instructor started off with a graphic explanation of the types of abuse children endure. I could relate. The verbal abuse. The neglect by withholding food. Physical abuse. I had lived through it all. That's why I was here. I wanted to help kids like me. But then the instructor said something that stopped me in my tracks. "Almost all abusive parents were themselves abused as a child. Your earliest lessons about parenting come from the family in which you grow up. Your family is the mirror of what you become."

If that's true, then I have no business even thinking about going down this path. No one should ever let a child near me,

not if I am doomed to become a mirror of my own father.
Becoming my father was and still is my greatest fear. I never
married in part because I did not want to take the chance of
repeating his mistakes. My whole motivation now for becoming a foster father was to provide a safe space for children.
*But what if I snap like my dad? What if I lose control and
lash out physically? I could never live with myself if that
happened. I should probably just forget about this.*

But I couldn't forget it. I could not go back to my comfortable life and ignore the fact that there were suffering children
right in my own neighborhood that I could help. And I knew
I could help them.

Once my initial panic died down, I reminded myself that
I was forty-three years old and that if I was going to become
my father, it would have happened by now. The MAPP class
forced me to confront my past once again, but I found it
healing. Now that I recognized the patterns handed down
to me from my own family, I could avoid them and be the
father I wish I'd had. Besides, my biological father was not
my only example. James showed me what a father was supposed to be. Through him I met other good families with
loving, supportive dads. The friends I made at the running
club in Kampala and through the US Embassy were also
good fathers. Once I came to the United States, I hung out
with Solomon's family and Derek's family and saw more
examples in their dads. Now I had a choice: Which example
was I going to follow? While we are all shaped by our past,
none of us are chained to it. None of us are predestined to
repeat the mistakes of the generations that came before. We
all have a choice about the type of person we will be. I was
lucky, after the age of fifteen, to have lived alongside living,

breathing examples of the man and father I wanted to be. That's what I was going to be.

I also came up with a test for myself to see if I was ready for the responsibility of being a father. After googling the hardest houseplants to keep alive, I went out and bought a zebra plant and a Boston fern. The way I saw it, if I couldn't keep a couple of plants alive, then I had no business taking at-risk kids into my home. Thankfully, both survived. *Okay*, I told myself, *I'm ready*.

We'll Call You in Thirty Minutes

Five months after my first meeting with Esther, she told me the good news. "Peter, you've passed everything. The background checks. The interviews. Your classes. The home study. Congratulations. You are now a licensed foster parent."

Those words were music to my ears. "That's wonderful. What happens now?" I asked.

"As soon as a child needs to be placed, we will call you," Esther said.

"So, what are we talking about, a week, maybe two?"

"We might call you in thirty minutes," Esther said.

I waited for her to laugh and say, "Not really." But she didn't laugh. She was serious. "Wait a minute. As in half an hour from right now?"

"Unfortunately, we have so few foster families available that the moment someone is licensed, we call. We have children who need to be placed at every hour of every day. Congratulations on the license, Peter. We will talk soon," Esther said.

"Okay," I said. "Whenever you need me, I'm ready."

I hung up the phone and looked around my house. I have never been married. I have never experienced the father's side of childbirth, but this is what it had to feel like. It was like my wife had come in to tell me her water had broken and the baby was on the way! I started rushing around my house, straightening up. My phone dinged with a text message. My heart jumped into my throat. *Is this it?* It wasn't. My email notification went off. Esther said she was going to call, but what if she emailed me instead? I checked it quickly. Nothing. I went into the kitchen to make myself something to eat, but I could not force food into my mouth. Through it all, I kept pacing and pacing and pacing, waiting for my phone to ring.

It rang. The caller ID said Esther. I took a deep breath. "Hello."

"Peter, are you ready?"

"I don't know. Do you think I am?" I asked. I didn't feel ready. Five months of classes? I think if I had taken five years of classes I still wouldn't have felt ready.

"You did everything you were required to do," Esther said.

"Okay, I guess I am then," I said, trying to sound confident. Inside I thought, *But you didn't answer my question.* I needed someone to tell me that I had this, that I could do this. But no one did. I have come to understand that every new parent feels this exact same way.

"We have a placement for you, a five-year-old Native American boy. I know you said that you were open to adoption, but that's not an option with him. We're not sure how long he will be with you. It could be a night or two, but it may be longer. One of our social workers is headed your way with him from Tulsa. It will probably take her a couple of hours to get to your house in the City." In Oklahoma, everyone calls Oklahoma City "the City."

"Okay," I said. "So, what should I do now?"

"I think you've done everything already. Just relax until he gets there," Esther said.

Yeah, that's easy for you to say, I thought.

I didn't relax. I went into my new child's room and made his bed. Then I straightened it. I went into my closet. *What should I wear?* I wondered. Then I looked in the mirror. *He's five. He won't care what I am wearing.* I went into the kitchen and made some snacks just in case he was hungry when he arrived. *What should I say when he first comes in? Hi, I'm Peter; I'm going to be your foster dad? Should I use the word* dad? *Won't that remind him of being ripped out of his home? I wonder if he has a dad at home.*

Questions like these ran through my head nonstop from the time I received Esther's call until a car pulled into my driveway. I went to the door. I heard the car doors open, then shut. Do I wait for them to knock? No, I should open the door now and welcome him. I opened the door as a little boy wearing a backpack walked up on my porch. "Hi, I'm Peter. I guess you are going to stay with me for a little while."

He nodded his head and muttered something like "Uh-huh."

"Okay, come on inside."

The boy walked in, and his eyes grew wide. "Whoa," he said. "You must be rich. This is the fanciest house I have ever seen."

I let out a nervous laugh. "No, not really."

The social worker came over and handed me his paperwork along with a black trash bag filled with his belongings.

Sadly, black trash bags are the universal standard luggage for foster children. "You look rich to him. We removed him from his grandmother's small, broken-down mobile home. She had twelve kids living there with her." She shook her head. "The conditions these kids have to live in . . . You never get used to it."

I understood better than she could have known. No wonder my brightly lit, quiet, sixteen-hundred-square-foot ranch house with new furniture and fresh paint looked like a mansion. I flashed back to the first time I had entered James's home. I thought he had to be the richest person on earth because of how nice his house was, even though I now understood he was anything but rich.

"Well," the social worker said, "I have a long drive in front of me and it's already late. Good luck."

"Uh, thank you," I said.

When the door closed behind her, I turned to this five-year-old boy looking up at me with wide eyes. It had to be the same way I had looked up at James and my teachers at Katweha. This child had to be as scared and uncomfortable in a nice place as I had been the first time I had gone into James's home. And what I felt in my heart had to be what James had felt toward me, and that was unconditional love. I did not know this child, but I was ready to do whatever I needed to do to help him.

Okay. Here we go.

fourteen

Full Circle

My first placement[1] was an angel—for all of two days. He came in that first night and asked two questions. The first: "Where do I sleep?" I took him into his room and showed him his bed. He looked up at me and said, "This is really for me?"

"For you and no one else."

He gave me a big smile.

His next question was "Can I have something to eat?" I took him over to the kitchen table, where I had a plate of snacks waiting for him. He ate a little, then asked for a glass of milk. I poured one for him, which he downed in an instant. "Can I have some more?" I poured a second glass. He downed it almost as fast as the first. "Can I have another?" he asked. *Have you been starving?* I wondered. But I didn't say anything except, "Of course. All that you want." He drank the third glass much more slowly. I don't know if he really wanted it or if he was testing me to see how much milk I actually had.

"You talk funny," he said.

"Yes. I am not from around here. I grew up in Uganda, a country in Africa."

"You sound like someone I know," he said.

"Really. Who?"

"I think it was someone in a cartoon."

I laughed. "Well, I hope he's one of the good guys."

"Yeah, he is."

It was very late when he arrived at my house, so after a small snack and his three glasses of milk, I told him it was time for bed. I took him over to the bathroom next to his bedroom. His eyes grew wide and looked all around like he'd never seen a bathroom so big and nice and clean. "This is for you to use," I said.

"For real?" he asked.

"Yes, for real."

He gave me a big smile. "I'm going to like it here," he said.

I went to bed that night and could barely sleep. I wondered if I had looked around James's house with the same wide eyes as my new foster son. When I first walked into James's home, I thought they had to be the richest people on earth. Now a little boy was curled up in a bed down the hall from me thinking the same thing. I couldn't believe how much food James's family had. When I went there, it was like I had died and gone to heaven. Now I was on the other side. My life had come full circle. I was James, and the little boy down the hall was me.

My first two days as a foster parent went so much easier than I ever thought possible. I knew this had to be too good to be true, but I let my mind think that I had been ready after all. I started to think that because I could relate in a very personal way to the trauma this child had gone through, he related to me in a way he couldn't with any other foster dad.

Then came the end of the second day. He was sitting next to a window, playing with my tablet, and he looked so angelic. This child was easy to love. But then I uttered the words that transformed my angel into something quite different. I told him, "It's time to put the tablet away and go to bed."

He ignored me and kept on playing. I walked over closer and repeated, "Okay. Tablet time is over. Now it is bedtime."

Again, he ignored me.

Finally, I reached out and took the tablet. "Listen, tablet time is over. You have to go to bed."

The moment I lifted the tablet out of his hand, the screaming began. He threw his head back against the window, one, two, three, four, five times. On the fifth blow, the window shattered, cutting his head, but the pain did not faze him. He kept on crying as I examined his head and cleaned up the blood from his minor scratches. I tried to reason with him. I tried to soothe him. Nothing I did made any difference. It was like my little boy had left the building. He had absolutely zero control over what he was doing.

He kept on crying uncontrollably for two solid hours. The whole time my head was spinning as I tried to figure out what to do. I kept looking over at the broken window. If we had been on a higher floor somewhere, he might have jumped. I didn't think about the time I almost threw Andrew out the window, but I should have. *What was I thinking? Why did I think I was ready for this?* I knew something had triggered his trauma, but I had no idea how to un-trigger it.

After two solid hours of screaming, he stopped and walked over to me with his arms held out. "Would you hold me?" he said.

"Of course, buddy." I pulled him up in my arms and held on tightly. He snuggled down close, and I have to tell you that was the most wonderful feeling in all the world. I had no idea what had just happened, how he had gone from screaming to cuddling up in my arms. Even if I knew, I probably wouldn't have understood it. His cries were the shrieks of a hurting child. I was thankful I was there to comfort him.

After resting in my arms for a few minutes, he raised up and asked, "Can I have a glass of milk?"

He downed a glass, wiped his mouth, and headed off to bed like nothing had happened.

This was not his last screaming fit. It happened at Chuck E. Cheese when I did not prepare him well ahead of time for our departure. It happened in the grocery store. Fits like this could come at any moment. No matter how many I went through, I never felt fully prepared for the next one when it happened.

My first placement stayed with me for six months before the Department of Child Services (DCS) moved him to the home of an aunt. I've kept in touch with the family. He's nearly nine now and doing well. I hope for his aunt's sake that he has outgrown his fits. But even through the fits, this was a boy who just wanted to be held, and I thank God I was there for him.

Can I Call You "Dad"?

In all my classes and training to become a foster dad, no one ever taught me how to say goodbye to my children when DCS shuffled them back to their biological parents or a family member. With my first child, I knew it was coming from the start. I counted on it, but that did not stop me from loving this little boy as a son. He started calling me "Dad" a few weeks after he came into my home. But "Dad" did not carry any real emotional weight for me when he first said it. I filled the Dad role for him. That's why he used the word. Still, when DCS moved him, I was not ready for him to leave. For six months, I poured myself 110 percent into being his father. Every hour of every day I cared for him and loved him and worried about him like any parent cares and loves and worries about their children. I always knew our arrangement was temporary, but I still was not prepared emotionally when one minute he was with me and the next he was gone.

Ten more children followed in rapid succession. The placements overlapped, with some staying months, others only weeks. I bought each one a houseplant to care for while they were with me, although I avoided Boston ferns and zebra plants. Instead, I found plants that required as little care as possible. My children had been through enough already. I didn't want to add to their trauma by having them kill a plant. When the time came for each child to leave, I kept their plant as a permanent reminder of them in my home. That didn't make saying goodbye any easier. I grieved each one when they left.

It never got easier to tell a child goodbye, only harder, especially with placement numbers ten and eleven. They stayed with me for nine months. During that time, the social workers assigned to the case told me that parental rights could possibly be terminated, which meant I might be able to adopt them. I wanted that more than anything. My children and I had bonded. I was their dad just as much as if we had been connected biologically. But then a judge made a ruling, and just like that, they went to live with a relative, leaving me with nothing but two houseplants to remember them by.

That last goodbye was more than I could take. Honestly, I did not think I could keep doing this. The pain was more than I could bear. Even though I knew the system was still filled with children who'd been pulled from their homes at no fault of their own, I wondered if I was the one to provide a home for them. I called my social worker, Esther, and told her I needed to take a break. "How long of a break do you need?" she asked.

"At least three months. Maybe more. Maybe forever. I'll let you know," I said.

That conversation took place on a Monday. Friday afternoon Esther called. I knew why she was calling.

"It's only been four days, Esther. I told you I need at least three months before I will even think about another placement," I said.

"I know, Peter, and I respect that, but we have a child that's been left at the hospital and I need to find a place for him just for the weekend. Monday morning I'll find another place for him, but it's Friday and I don't have any other options."

"I can't," I said.

"Peter, I promise you that it is only for the weekend. Come Monday, he's gone," Esther said.

"These placements never just last a weekend. I cannot open up my heart to another child, not right now."

"I don't have any other place to take him," Esther said.

Against my better judgment, I finally said, "Okay, but only until Monday morning."

"You have my word," Esther said.

A short time later, Esther arrived at my home with an eleven-year-old boy. I kept my guard up. I refused to let myself build any sort of attachment with him.

Esther left. I showed him around my house and took him into the room where he would stay for the next two nights. "You may call me Mr. Peter, if you'd like," I told him.

Without skipping a beat, the boy looked up at me and said, "May I call you 'Dad' instead?"

His answer caught me completely off guard. In all my previous eleven placements, it always took weeks, sometimes months, for children to start calling me "Dad." Without even thinking, I blurted out, "*Hell*, no."

He sort of jumped back like he knew he'd done something wrong, but he had no idea what it was.

"I apologize," I said. "I should not have sworn at you. You're only going to be here for a couple of nights, so let's just stick with Mr. Peter, okay?"

He shook his head. "Since I am eleven years old, I was told that I can choose who my father should be, and I'm choosing you to be my dad."

Oh my, does he have any idea what this conversation is doing to me? I just had two children who chose me to be their dad, and they got ripped out of my arms. I cannot go there again . . . especially after knowing each other for only twenty minutes! "Uhhhh," I stammered, "can we not go there right now? Asking that question right now is inappropriate. You're only here for the weekend."

"Well, can I call you 'Dad'?" he asked again.

"No," I said and ended the conversation.

On Monday morning, Esther came to pick him up just like she had promised. She and I sat down at my kitchen table to finish up the paperwork involved when a child leaves a foster family. "So, what's his story?" I asked now that I felt like I could safely do so. After all, this child was about to leave, and I'd never see him again. I wanted to know how he ended up at a hospital and then suddenly needed an emergency placement.

"He came into the foster care system when he was eighteen months old," she said. That made me think that he had bounced from one family to another for the past ten years. "He was placed with a family at that time, and they ended up adopting him when he was four. For nine years, they were the only family he ever knew, but on Friday they dropped him off at a hospital and never came back. They did not say goodbye to him. Instead, they just signed away their parental rights and left him without telling anyone why."

Immediately, I went back to my own experience as a child. My father did not abandon me, at least not physically, but he had emotionally and in every other way. I glanced over at the boy watching television in my living room while Esther and I talked. Anger swelled up inside me. "How could anyone do that to this child?" I asked. "Who could do such a thing?"

"I don't know," Esther replied.

"What's going to happen to him now?" I asked.

"He'll probably end up in a group home," she said.

I looked back at this boy. *Abandoned, like he was a dog the family didn't want anymore. How . . . ?* And then it hit me: I was about to do the same thing. He told me he wanted me to be his father, but I rejected him. From the beginning of my journey as a foster dad, all I wanted was to be a father, not temporarily but for the rest of my life and the rest of my child's life. That's why saying goodbye had always been so difficult. How could I say goodbye now?

"Give me his paperwork," I said. "You don't need to put him in a group home. He has a home here, with me."

"His parental rights have been terminated, which means I still need to find him a permanent home with parents willing to adopt him," she said.

"Yes. You've found that already," I said.

Just over a year and a half later, that boy who came into my home as a weekend placement stood with me before a judge and we heard the sweetest words ever uttered: "Your adoption is complete. Congratulations." Anthony was now officially my son, and I was simply a father, without the word *foster* in front of it.

Words That Hurt, Words That Heal

Becoming a dad made me think back even more on my own father. I no longer feared becoming a mirror image of him, but I could not stop thinking about the example he had set. Over thirty years later, I could still hear his words:

> You are worthless.
>
> You are garbage.
>
> A dog is more valuable than you because at least a dog can do something.
>
> You will never amount to anything.
>
> I wish you were dead.

I was proud of the fact that I had proved every one of my father's words false, and yet, the power of those words still came back when I least expected it and haunted me. His words have stuck with me for a lifetime. Thankfully, his were not the only words I heard.

I never heard any positive words from a man in my life until James told me I had potential. I've already written how those words sparked something inside me. But that was not the only time he spoke words of affirmation into my life. The biggest impact came about two or three years after James rescued me from the streets. I was a guest in his home during vacation, and he asked me to come with him to run an errand. We walked out to his Land Cruiser, and I instinctively opened a back door. In Africa, culturally, the front seats of a vehicle are reserved for family. Before I could get into the car, James said, "Why don't you get in the front seat, Peter? It's just the two of us."

I shook my head. "I'm fine back here."

"No, Peter, get in the front."

"But only family or someone really special rides up front," I said quietly.

"Peter," he said, "you *are* special, especially to us." No one had ever called me special before. The moment had such an impact on me that when we returned to his home, I went into my room and wrote the word *special* in a notebook. Another time James told me I was brave for making it through all the things I'd endured in life. In fact, he said that to me a lot. *Brave* went in my notebook.

From that point forward, when people spoke words of affirmation to me, I put them in the same notebook and carried it around with me. When I became a father, that notebook became the guide for how I spoke to my children. Every single day I make sure my children hear me say to them these words I hope they never forget:

You matter.

You belong.

You are loved.

You are seen.

You are chosen.

You are a gift.

You are not alone.

You are enough.

You are heard.

You are brave.

You are special.

You are known.

These aren't just words. Children who come through the foster care system find themselves shuffled about, from one placement to the next, everything they own stuffed into a black garbage bag. When that reality becomes your life, no one has to tell you that you don't matter and that you don't belong. You live that reality. You become invisible, a throwaway child no one seems to want, a child with no one upon whom you can depend. They need a place to belong. They need someone who sees them, who hears them, who not only says they matter but also treats them like they do. These are some of the bravest children—make that some of the bravest people—I have ever met, and I am not shy about telling them that.

Because my children are children, we have days when they don't want to listen to me. I speak, and they get angry and sulk off to their room. They don't want to see me for a while, but there is someone in the house they always want to spend time with: our dog, Simba. I brought Simba into my home not long after Anthony came to live with me. They say dogs are man's best friend, but they are really a child's best friend. When Anthony or one of my other children wants nothing to do with me, they usually cuddle with the dog or take Simba to their room. That is why I had these same words of affirmation printed on the dog's bandana. Even when the kids shut me out, they can read these powerful words hanging around Simba's neck. The impact is the same.

Children in the foster care system aren't the only ones who need to hear these words. Every child needs to know they are loved and that they belong. Every child needs to know they are chosen and that they are a gift. For that matter, every adult needs to hear these words. I grew up with a hole in my heart carved out by my father's words. Choosing to forgive him did not make that hole go away. James telling me I had potential filled a little of that hole. Friends in the dorms who accepted me even when my life was a mess helped fill that hole. The teacher at Katweha who told me I was too smart not to push myself to do my very best filled part of that hole. Semwo and Josh and other friends from Makerere University who accepted me and treated me as an equal filled a little more of that hole. Strangers from England who cared so much about me that they helped give me an opportunity to come and study and see more of the world filled that hole. Friends and family and everyone who has touched my life in a positive way has helped fill that hole.

That's what I hope reading my story can do for you. I hope you have heard in these pages the same words of affirmation. You are enough. You are a gift. You can make a difference if you will be brave and take steps of faith, believing you matter.

Thousands upon thousands of hurting and vulnerable children are hoping someone will take those steps. In the middle of the adoption process with Anthony, I accepted a job with another child advocacy group. The new job moved us to Charlotte, North Carolina. Right after we moved, I contacted the state's Child Protective Services to see if I could transfer my foster care license from Oklahoma. I did not like their answer: no. I had to go through the entire licensing process again. It would have been easy for me to tell them to forget it. After all, I was in the process of adopting my son. I could tell myself that he needed all my attention and easily justify no longer doing foster care.

But I couldn't do that. I went through the process again. And just like in Oklahoma, my phone rings constantly about children who need a family.

As I write these words today, 750 children in my community alone need a foster family; only 70 foster families are available—70 families for 750 children. The same scenario plays out across every city, county, and state in the United States. Children need homes, but far too few people are willing to step up and say, "I'll do it." I can't tell you how many times someone has told me, "I could never do what you do."

My response is simple: "Why not?"

Why not?

Children do not choose to be born to drug-addicted mothers. Children do not choose to grow up in a neglectful family any more than I chose to be born in a poor village to a father who did not want me. Children do not choose to go into foster care, but we have a choice. We can choose to make a difference in the lives of vulnerable children. Some people think it takes some sort of special call from God to become a foster parent. I disagree. All it takes is knowing there is a need and knowing you can do something to meet it.

Even foster parents need people to come around them and help them. It seems like almost every day I have to take one of my kids to a hearing or a visitation or therapy along with all the normal kid things like school and sports. Just imagine the difference we can make by taking a meal to a foster family once a week or volunteering to help their children with their homework. I have weeks when I don't have time to mow my yard. If someone came and did that for me, I'd feel like they were an angel sent from heaven. Someone once said that it takes a village to raise a child. Foster families usually feel outside that village. We can change that. Everyone can do something.

For years, I thought that I could make a difference in the lives of hurting children from a distance. I hate to think what may have happened to me if James had done that. He did more than provide a way for me to go to school. He welcomed me into his family, even when I had trouble staying with them. The love James and Martha expressed to me by accepting me for who I was and looking beyond my trauma to see the real me changed my life. I pray I can do the same for the children who come into my home.

Just like when the other couples in my MAPP class looked at me funny, I still get strange looks from people when I'm out with my children. Some have even called the police to report me. That's probably because most of the children who have come into my home do not look like me. Children don't have to look like me for me to love them and for them to love me back. A family is more than blood. It is a decision we make to love one another unconditionally, even when that love is not reciprocated.

I have many, many stories I can tell about my life as a dad, enough stories to fill two or three books. Perhaps, someday, when the kids are grown, they, too, will go full circle and do for other children what I have attempted to do for them. They might go on to tell their own stories of hope and purpose.

The world is filled with children who were just like I was. My entire life's work is to help others realize they are loved, they are chosen, they are heard, and they are known. All it took to turn my hopelessness upside down was one brave step on my part and another man's kindness. I found the courage to run away from a life of destitution and to try the opportunities that presented themselves. James saw my potential and offered me a new path. The combination of bravery and love can make all the difference in the world. It did for me. There is a world filled with children waiting for you to make a choice. Their lives will never be the same.

Choose to be brave. Choose to love.

Acknowledgments

I'm deeply grateful for Mark Tabb and his skill in understanding my world, asking hard questions, and finding the right words to express my life's story with passion and thoughtfulness.

To Andrea Vinley Converse for starting the journey and coming alongside me to bring things into focus.

To the Baker Publishing Group, who took me in as family and commits to doing meaningful work every day.

Thank you, Derek Breuninger, for helping me embrace and learn the ways of my new country.

Endless gratitude to Jason Johnson for showing me how to walk the talk.

Thank you, Andrea and Bradley Veazey, for showing me how to love unconditionally.

To the Yancey family for welcoming me into their home and seeing me through the highs and lows all these years.

To all my primary teachers who did not see a hopeless kid but cheered for and guided a kid with potential.

To my agent and friend, Annette Brashler Bourland, for her friendship, unwavering faith in me, and constant support throughout this process that began years ago.

To James and Martha and their children for rescuing me and seeing potential when I could not see it in myself.

To my mother for teaching me values and principles that helped me survive and still guide me to be the best human I can be.

To my father, who helped me understand the depth of grace and mercy.

Huge thanks to my children for letting me be their dad—something I dreamt of becoming since I was a little boy.

Notes

Chapter 2 Survival Mode

1. In Uganda and other parts of Africa, your last name is not a family name but something bestowed on you by your parents.
2. Pronounced Hobby.

Chapter 3 Seeking Happiness

1. I have changed her name to protect her and her family's privacy.

Chapter 4 Surprised by Kindness

1. This is not his actual name. I changed it along with the names of his wife and children to protect their privacy.

Chapter 6 First Flicker of Hope

1. That is, soccer.

Chapter 14 Full Circle

1. Legally I cannot share the names or ages of my children while they are in the foster care system. However, that does not apply to my son Anthony whom I have formally adopted.

Peter Mutabazi is the founder of Now I Am Known, an organization that supplies resources to support vulnerable children, increasing knowledge and awareness of how to make a life-changing difference in local communities. Peter is a passionate international speaker and advocate and has appeared in various media outlets. Peter has become Dad to countless foster children and his own adopted kids, along with two dogs. The family resides in North Carolina. For more information, visit: www.nowiamknown.com and follow Peter @fosterdadflipper and @nowiamknown.

CONNECT
with PETER

To find out more about how you can support
kids in foster care and other vulnerable children,
connect with Peter's organization at

NowIAmKnown.com

FOLLOW PETER ON SOCIAL MEDIA

 Peter Mutabazi Foster Dad    FosterDadFlippr

 fosterdadflipper   nowiamknown